Making Words Fifth Grade

50 Hands-On Lessons for Teaching Prefixes, Suffixes, and Roots

Patricia M. Cunningham
Wake Forest University

Dorothy P. Hall
Wake Forest University

Boston • New York • San Francisco
Mexico City • Montreal • Toronto • London • Madrid • Munich • Paris
Hong Kong • Singapore • Tokyo • Cape Town • Sydney

Executive Editor: Aurora Martínez Ramos
Series Editorial Assistant: Kara Kikel
Marketing Manager: Danae April
Production Editor: Annette Joseph
Editorial Production Service: Lynda Griffiths
Composition Buyer: Linda Cox
Manufacturing Buyer: Linda Morris
Electronic Composition: Denise Hoffman
Interior Design: Denise Hoffman
Cover Designer: Kristina Mose-Libon

For Professional Development resources, visit www.allynbaconmerrill.com.

Between the time website information is gathered and then published, it is not unusual for some sites to have closed. Also, the transcription of URLs can result in typographical errors. The publisher would appreciate notification where these errors occur so that they may be corrected in subsequent editions.

ISBN-10: 0-205-58102-1
ISBN-13: 978-0-205-58102-3

Printed in the United States of America

10 9 8 7 6 5 4 3 2 1   12 11 10 09 08

Photos: Dorothy P. Hall.

**Allyn & Bacon
is an imprint of**

www.pearsonhighered.com

Pat   *Dottie*

Patricia M. Cunningham

From the day I entered first grade, I knew I wanted to be a first-grade teacher. In 1965, I graduated from the University of Rhode Island and began my teaching career teaching first grade in Key West, Florida. For the next several years, I taught a variety of grades and worked as a curriculum coordinator and special reading teacher in Florida and Indiana. From the very beginning, I worried about the children who struggled in learning to read and so I devised a variety of alternative strategies to teach them to read. In 1974, I received my Ph.D. in Reading Education from the University of Georgia.

I developed the Making Words activity while working with Title I teachers in North Carolina, where I was the Director of Reading for Alamance County Schools. I have been the Director of Elementary Education at Wake Forest University in Winston-Salem, North Carolina, since 1980 and have worked with numerous teachers to develop hands-on, engaging ways to teach phonics and spelling. In 1991, I wrote *Phonics They Use: Words for Reading and Writing*, which is currently available in its fifth edition. Along with Richard Allington, I also wrote *Classrooms that Work* and *Schools that Work*.

Dottie Hall and I have worked together on many projects. In 1989, we began developing the Four Blocks Framework, a comprehensive approach to literacy that is used in many schools in the United States and Canada. Dottie and I have produced many books together, including the first *Making Words* books and the *Month by Month Phonics* books. These *Making Words* for grade levels kindergarten to fifth grade are in response to requests by teachers across the years to have Making Words lessons with a scope and sequence tailored to their various grade levels. We hope you and your students will enjoy these Making Words lessons and we would love to hear your comments and suggestions.

Dorothy P. Hall

I always wanted to teach young children. After graduating from Worcester State College in Massachusetts, I taught first and second grades. Two years later, I moved to North Carolina, where I continued teaching in the primary grades. Many children I worked with in the newly integrated schools struggled in learning to read. Wanting to increase my knowledge, I received my M.Ed. and Ed.D. in Reading from the University of North Carolina at Greensboro. I also worked at Wake Forest University, where I met and began to work with Pat Cunningham.

After three years of teaching at the college level I returned to the public schools and taught third and fourth grades and served as a reading and curriculum coordinator for my school district. At this time Pat Cunningham and I began to collaborate on a number of projects. In 1989, we developed the Four Blocks Framework, a comprehensive approach to literacy in grades 1, 2, and 3, which we called Big Blocks. Later, we expanded the program to include kindergarten, calling it Building Blocks. By 1999, Pat and I had written four *Making Words* books, a series of *Month by Month Phonics* books, and *The Teacher's Guide to Four Blocks*, and I retired from the school system to devote more time to consulting and writing. I also went back to work at Wake Forest University, where I taught courses in reading, children's literature, and language arts instruction for elementary education students.

Today, I am Director of the Four Blocks Center at Wake Forest University and enjoy working with teachers and administrators around the country presenting workshops on Four Blocks, Building Blocks, guided reading strategies, and phonics instruction. I have also written several books with teachers. One request Pat and I have had for a number of years is to revise the *Making Words* by grade level and include a scope and sequence for the phonics instruction taught. Here it is—Enjoy!

Our thanks to those who reviewed *Making Words Fifth Grade:* Cheryl Dick, Nixa R-II School District (MO); Jane E. Harriger, Buchanan Elementary School (Grand Rapids Public Schools, MI); and Melissa A. Rareshide, Pinebrook Elementary School (NC).

Contents

Introduction   1

Lesson 1 ● **watermelons**   9
Lesson Focus: **er/est**, meaning more and most
re, meaning back or again

Lesson 2 ● **grandchildren**   10
Lesson Focus: **er**, meaning person or thing that does something

Lesson 3 ● **cheerleaders**   12
Lesson Focus: **er**, meaning person or thing that does something
re, meaning back or again

Lesson 4 ● **earthquakes**   14
Lesson Focus: **er**, meaning person or thing that does something
re, meaning back or again

Lesson 5 ● **fingerprints**   16
Lesson Focus: **er/est**, meaning more and most
er, meaning person or thing that does something
re, meaning back or again

Lesson 6 ● **quarterbacks**   18
Lesson Focus: **er**, meaning person or thing that does something

Lesson 7 ● **searchlight**   20
Lesson Focus: **er/est**, meaning more and most
ist, meaning person

Lesson 8 ● **planetarium**   22
Lesson Focus: **un**, meaning not or opposite
im, meaning in
re, meaning back or again
er, meaning person or thing that does something

Lesson 9 • **unfriendly**   24

Lesson Focus: **un**, meaning not or opposite

re, meaning back or again

ly, changing part of speech

y, changing part of speech

Lesson 10 • **unfriendliest**   26

Lesson Focus: **un**, meaning not or opposite

under, meaning under or less

re, meaning back or again

er, meaning person or thing that does something

Lesson 11 • **unfriendliness**   28

Lesson Focus: **un**, meaning not or opposite

under, meaning under or less

re, meaning back or again

less, meaning less or without

ness, changing part of speech

Lesson 12 • **personality**   30

Lesson Focus: **er/ist**, meaning person or thing that does something

re, meaning back or again

ly, changing part of speech

Lesson 13 • **carelessly**   32

Lesson Focus: **less**, meaning less or without

ly, changing part of speech

y, changing part of speech

re, meaning back or again

Lesson 14 • **meaningless**   34

Lesson Focus: **less**, meaning less or without

ness, changing part of speech

Lesson 15 • **mercilessly**   36

Lesson Focus: **er**, meaning person or thing that does something

re, meaning back or again

less, meaning less or without

ly, changing part of speech

y, changing part of speech

Lesson 16 • **gracefully**   38
Lesson Focus: **ful**, meaning full or with
re, meaning back or again
ly, changing part of speech
y, changing part of speech

Lesson 17 • **unfortunately**   39
Lesson Focus: **un**, meaning not or opposite
en, changing part of speech
ly, changing part of speech

Lesson 18 • **unworkable**   40
Lesson Focus: **able**, meaning able to
un, meaning not or opposite
er, meaning person or thing that does something
en, changing part of speech

Lesson 19 • **unbreakable**   41
Lesson Focus: **un**, meaning not or opposite
en, meaning to make
able, meaning able to
er, meaning person or thing that does something

Lesson 20 • **undesirable**   42
Lesson Focus: **un**, meaning not or opposite
dis, meaning not or opposite
en, meaning to make
re, meaning back or again
able, meaning able to
er, meaning person or thing that does

Lesson 21 • **questionable**   44
Lesson Focus: **un**, meaning opposite
en, meaning to make
able, meaning able to
tion, changing part of speech

Lesson 22 • **unpredictable**   46
Lesson Focus: **un**, meaning not or opposite
re, meaning back or again
in, meaning not or opposite
able, meaning able to

Lesson 23 • **uncomfortable**   48

Lesson Focus: **un**, meaning not or opposite

re, meaning back or again

ful, meaning full or with

able, meaning able to

Lesson 24 • **undependable**   49

Lesson Focus: **un**, meaning not or opposite

able, meaning able to

re, meaning back or again

en, meaning to make

Lesson 25 • **disagreeable**   50

Lesson Focus: **dis**, meaning opposite

er, meaning person or thing that does something

re, meaning back or again

able, meaning able to

Lesson 26 • **disagreement**   52

Lesson Focus: **er/est**, meaning more and most

dis, meaning opposite

ee, meaning person

ment, changing part of speech

Lesson 27 • **reinforcements**   54

Lesson Focus: **er/est**, meaning more and most

re, meaning back or again

er, meaning person or thing that does something

ment, changing part of speech

Lesson 28 • **imperfectly**   55

Lesson Focus: **ly**, changing part of speech

y, changing part of speech

re, meaning back or again

im, meaning not or opposite

Lesson 29 • **irresponsible**   56

Lesson Focus: **less**, meaning less or without

re, meaning back or again

er, meaning person or thing that does something

ir, meaning opposite

ible, meaning able to

Lesson 30 ● **misunderstand**   58
Lesson Focus: **dis**, meaning not or opposite
         in, meaning not or opposite
         un, meaning not or opposite
         mis, meaning wrong or badly
         er/est, meaning more/most

Lesson 31 ● **misunderstood**   59
Lesson Focus: **dis**, meaning not or opposite
         mis, meaning wrong or badly
         en, changing part of speech

Lesson 32 ● **interactively**   60
Lesson Focus: **inter**, meaning between
         in, meaning not or opposite
         ee, meaning person
         ly, changing part of speech

Lesson 33 ● **interactions**   62
Lesson Focus: **er/est**, meaning more and most
         re, meaning back or again
         inter, meaning between
         in, meaning not or opposite
         er/or/ist, meaning person or thing that does something
         tion, changing part of speech

Lesson 34 ● **international**   63
Lesson Focus: **inter**, meaning between
         in, meaning not or opposite
         al, changing part of speech
         tion, changing part of speech

Lesson 35 ● **mysteriously**   64
Lesson Focus: **mis**, meaning wrong or badly
         y, changing part of speech
         ly, changing part of speech
         ous, changing part of speech

Lesson 36 • **dangerously**   65
    Lesson Focus: **un**, meaning not or opposite
                  re, meaning back or again
                  ly, changing part of speech
                  ous, changing part of speech

Lesson 37 • **independently**   66
    Lesson Focus: **in**, meaning not or opposite (independent)
                  in, meaning in (indent)
                  en, meaning to make
                  y, changing part of speech
                  ly, changing part of speech

Lesson 38 • **dependability**   68
    Lesson Focus: **in**, meaning not or opposite
                  en, changing part of speech
                  y, changing part of speech
                  ly, changing part of speech

Lesson 39 • **encouragement**   69
    Lesson Focus: **er/or**, meaning person
                  re, meaning back or again
                  en, meaning to make
                  ment, changing part of speech

Lesson 40 • **arrangements**   70
    Lesson Focus: **er/est**, meaning more/most
                  re, meaning back or again
                  er, meaning person
                  ment, changing part of speech

Lesson 41 • **replacements**   72
    Lesson Focus: **er/est**, meaning more/most
                  re, meaning back or again
                  er, meaning person
                  al, changing part of speech
                  ment, changing part of speech

Lesson 42 ● **underweight**   74

Lesson Focus: **under**, meaning under or less

re, meaning back or again

er, meaning person or thing that does something

er, meaning more

Lesson 43 ● **underestimate**   76

Lesson Focus: **under**, meaning under or less

re, meaning back or again

ee, meaning person

mis, meaning wrong or badly

en, meaning to make

Lesson 44 ● **overestimate**   78

Lesson Focus: **over**, meaning over or more

er, meaning person or thing that does something

Lesson 45 ● **performances**   79

Lesson Focus: **en**, meaning to make

er, meaning person or thing that does something

ance, changing part of speech

Lesson 46 ● **resistance**   80

Lesson Focus: **er/est**, meaning more/most

re, meaning back or again

en, meaning to make

er/ee, meaning person

ance, changing part of speech

Lesson 47 ● **disappearance**   81

Lesson Focus: **dis**, meaning not or opposite

pre, meaning before

en, meaning to make

er, meaning person or thing that does something

ance, changing part of speech

Lesson 48 ● **predictions/description**   82

Lesson Focus: **er/or**, meaning person

er/est, meaning more/most

tion, changing part of speech

Contents

Lesson 49 • reproduction   84

        Lesson Focus: **er/or**, meaning person

                       un, meaning not or opposite

                       re, meaning back or again

                       tion, changing part of speech

Lesson 50 • contradictions   86

        Lesson Focus: **or/ist**, meaning person

                       tion, changing part of speech

• **Reproducible Letter Strips**   87

• **Reproducible Take-Home Sheet**   107

Introduction

Many teachers first discovered Making Words in the first edition of *Phonics They Use*, which was published in 1991. Since then, teachers around the world have used Making Words lessons to help students discover how our spelling system works. Making Words lessons are an example of a type of instruction called guided discovery. In order to truly learn and retain strategies, learners must discover them. But many students do not make discoveries about words on their own. In Making Words lessons, students are guided to make those discoveries.

Making Words is a popular activity with both teachers and students. Students love manipulating letters to make words and figuring out the secret word that can be made with all the letters. While students are having fun making words, they are also learning important information about phonics and spelling.

Teaching a Making Words Lesson

Every Making Words lesson has three parts. First, students manipulate the letters to *make* words. This part of the lesson uses a spelling approach to help students learn the complex letter combinations they need to know to spell English words. In the second part of the lesson, students *sort* words according to patterns. In fifth grade, the patterns students need to learn are prefixes, suffixes, and roots, and how these word parts go together to form related words. We end each lesson by helping students *transfer* what they have learned to reading and spelling new words. Students learn how the related words they sorted help them read and spell lots of other words.

Each Making Words lesson begins with short words and moves to longer, more complex words. The last word is always the secret word—a word that can be made with all the letters. As students arrange the letters, a student who has successfully made a word manipulates the pocket-chart letters or overhead transparency letters to make the word. Students who don't have the word made correctly quickly fix their word so that they're ready for the next word. In fifth grade, each lesson consists of 15 to 20 words, including the secret word that can be made with all the letters.

In Part Two of a Making Words lesson, students sort the words into patterns. In *Making Words Fifth Grade*, all words in each lesson have one or more related words—that is, words with the same root. Students sort the words into related words and, with guidance from the teacher, construct a sentence to show the relationship of these words.

The final, and most important, step of each Making Words lesson is transfer. After words are sorted according to related words, students are guided to spell new words based on these related words. Here is an example of how you might conduct a Making Words lesson and cue the students to the changes and words you want them to make. (This lesson is #8 in *Making Words Fifth Grade*.)

Beginning the Lesson

The students all have a letter strip with these letters: a a e i u l m n p r t

One student is assigned the job of "letter manipulator" for today's lesson. As students make each word at their desks, the teacher calls on a student who has the word made correctly to spell aloud the letters in that word. The letter manipulator moves the letters on the overhead so that everyone has a visual image against which to check their spelling. (You can make clear letter tiles by cutting a sheet of transparency film into small squares, then writing the letters for the lesson on the squares, or you can copy the letter strips at the back of this book on a transparency and have the letter manipulator cut the letters on the plastic strip apart.)

Students tear or cut the letters apart and arrange them in alphabetical order—vowels first and consonants next.

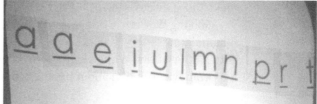

The words the students are going to make are written on index cards. These words will be placed in the pocket chart or along the chalk ledge and will be used for the Sort and Transfer parts of the lesson.

Part One • Making Words

The teacher begins the lesson by telling students what word to make and how many letters each word requires. She or he gives a sentence for each word to clarify meaning.

> "Use 4 letters to spell the word **real**. The creatures in the movie were animated but they looked very **real**."

Find someone with **real** spelled correctly and have that student spell **real** aloud so that the letter manipulator can spell **real** with the transparency letters.

> "Use 4 letters to spell **ripe**. We pick strawberries when they are **ripe**."

> "Spell another 4-letter word, **mine**. Would you like to work deep down under the earth in a coal **mine**?"

> "Let's spell one more 4-letter word, **time**. What **time** do we go to lunch?"

> "Add 1 letter to **time** to spell **timer**. I put the cookies in the oven and set the **timer** for 15 minutes."

> "Use 5 letters again to spell **miner**. I am claustrophobic so I would not be a good coal **miner**."

(Quickly call on someone with the correct spelling to spell the word aloud for the letter manipulator. Keep the pace brisk. Choose your struggling readers to spell words aloud when easy words are being spelled and your advanced readers when harder words are being made.)

"Use 5 letters to spell **ripen**. The strawberries are just beginning to **ripen**."

"Use 5 letters to spell **paint**. We all love to **paint** in art class."

"Use 5 letters to spell **plant**. In the spring we will **plant** flowers in our garden."

"Add 1 letter to **plant** to spell **planet**. Mars is called the red **planet**."

"Use 6 letters to spell **unreal**. Everyone said that watching the tornado touch down felt very **unreal**."

"Use 6 letters to spell **unripe**. Strawberries do not taste good when they are **unripe**."

"Use 7 letters to spell **planter**. I plant spring flowers in a hanging **planter**."

"Use the same letters in **planter** to spell **replant**. Every year I **replant** the shrubs that die during the winter."

"Change the first 2 letters in **replant** to spell **implant**. If your heart does not have a steady beat, doctors can **implant** a pacemaker into your body to regulate your heartbeat."

"Use 7 letters to spell **painter**. The **painter** is coming next week to paint the house."

"Use the same 7 letters in **painter** to spell **repaint**. After the storm, the roof leaked and we had to **repaint** the kitchen."

"I have just one word left. It is the secret word you can make with all your letters. Move your letters around and see if you can figure out the word that can be spelled using all the letters. You have 1 minute to try to figure out the secret word and then I will give you clues."

(Give the students one minute to figure out the secret word. Then give clues if needed. "Our secret word today is related to the word **planet**. Start with the word **planet** and add your other letters to it.")

Let someone who figures it out go to the overhead and spell the secret word: **planetarium**.

Part Two • Sort Words into Patterns

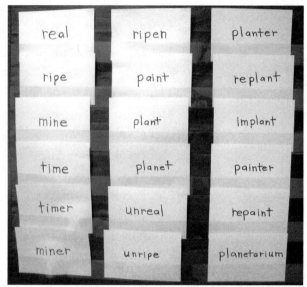

Draw students' attention to the words on the index cards and have the words pronounced. Remind students that related words are words that share a root word and meaning.

Choose a set of related words and model for students how to use related words in sentences to show how they are related. (Choose the most complex set of words to model.)

plant   planter   replant   implant

"A **planter** is a container you plant things in. When you **replant** something, you **plant** it again. When you **implant** something, you **plant** it in something or somebody."

"The **er** suffix can be a person or a thing. **Re** is a prefix that sometimes means again. **Im** is a prefix that sometimes means in."

Let volunteers choose other sets of related words and help them construct sentences and explain how the prefixes and suffixes change the root words.

paint   painter   repaint

"A **painter** is a person who **paints**. When you **repaint** something, you **paint** it again."

"**Er** is a suffix that sometimes means the person who does something. **Re** is a prefix that sometimes means again."

ripe   ripen   unripe

"The strawberries are starting to **ripen** and will soon be **ripe** enough to eat. **Unripe** strawberries taste terrible!"

"The suffix **en** changes how a word can be used in a sentence. The prefix **un** often turns a word into the opposite meaning."

real   unreal

"When you see something this is actually happening it is **real** but sometimes things are so strange they seem **unreal**."

"The prefix **un** changes **real** into the opposite meaning."

time   timer

"To **time** the cookies baking, we set the **timer**."

"The suffix **er** sometimes means a thing."

mine   miner

"A **miner** is a person who works in a **mine**."

"The suffix **er** sometimes means a person."

planet   planetarium

"You can see all the different **planets** and how they move at a **planetarium**."

"Other words that end in **ium** and mean places are **aquarium**, **terrarium**, **auditorium**, **gymnasium**, and **stadium**."

Sorting the related words, using sentences that show how they are related, and explaining how prefixes and suffixes affect meaning or change how words can be used in a sentence is a crucial part of each Making Words lesson in fifth grade. Students often need help in explaining how the prefixes and suffixes work. For less common prefixes and suffixes, such as **ium**, it is helpful to point out other words students may know that begin or end with that word part.

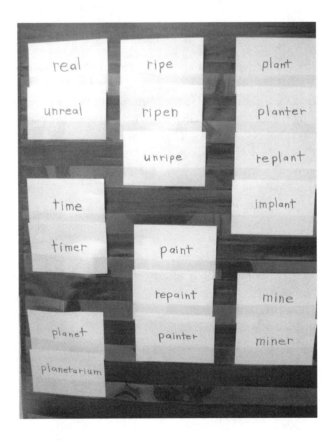

Part Three • Transfer

The transfer step is the most important step of the lesson because it is when we teach students how the prefixes, suffixes, and roots they are learning help them read and spell lots of other words. Once we have sorted all the words into related word sets, we say five or six new words and have students decide which word parts these words share with our related words and how they will help the students spell them. It is very important to make this a learning experience rather than a test. Make sure everyone knows how to spell the new part of the transfer word and which related words will help before letting anyone write the word.

Ask the students to number a sheet of paper from 1 to 6. Pronounce a word that follows the pattern of some of the related words.

Have the students use **unripe** and **unreal** to spell other words that begin with **un**. Give them help to spell the root word if needed.

unfair   unpainted

Let volunteers say a sentence that shows the meaning relationship between **fair**, **unfair**; **painted**, **unpainted**.

Have the students use **repaint** and **replant** to spell other words that begin with **re**. Give them help to spell the root word if needed.

rebuild   refill

Let volunteers say a sentence that shows the meaning relationship between **build**, **rebuild**; **fill**, **refill**.

Have the students use **painter**, **planter**, **miner**, and **timer** to spell other words that end with **er**, meaning person or thing. Give them help to spell the root word if needed. Point out the spelling change—drop **e**—if necessary.

leader   driver

Let volunteers say a sentence that shows the meaning relationship between **lead**, **leader**; **drive**, **driver**.

We hope this sample lesson has helped you see how a fifth-grade Making Words lesson works and how Making Words lessons help fifth-graders learn how prefixes and suffixes affect the meanings of root words and how combining word parts help students spell lots of other words.

Zannie Murphy
1. unfair
2. unpainted
3. rebuild
4. refill
5. leader
6. driver

Introduction

Spelling and Decoding Skills Taught in Making Words Fifth-Grade Lessons

Making Words Fifth Grade contains 50 lessons that teach the most common roots, prefixes, and suffixes. In addition to learning to decode and spell words with these prefixes and suffixes, students learn how these prefixes and suffixes change the meanings of words and how these words are used in sentences.

Prefixes

The common prefixes taught in *Making Words Fifth Grade* are:

un, meaning not or opposite (unhappy, unfinished)

in/im/ir, meaning not or opposite (incorrect, impossible, irregular)

dis, meaning not or opposite (disappear, disagree)

re, meaning back or again (return, rewrite)

in/im, meaning in (inmate, implant)

pre, meaning before (prepay, preview)

mis, meaning wrong or badly (misuse, misspell)

en, meaning to make (ensure, endear)

under, meaning under or less (underweight, underestimate)

over, meaning over or more (overweight, overestimate)

inter, meaning between (international, interact)

Suffixes

Suffixes sometimes change meanings of words and sometimes change how the word can be used in a sentence. Often, when a suffix is added, the root word has a spelling change. Spelling changes—consonant doubling, **y** changing to **i** and dropping **e**—should be pointed out to students during the sorting and transfer step of each lesson if students still need support in consistently applying these spelling changes in their writing. The common suffixes taught are:

er/est, meaning more/most (happier, happiest)

ful, meaning full or with (careful, meaningful)

less, meaning less or without (careless, meaningless)

able/ible, meaning able to (removable, visible)

er, meaning person or thing that does something (reporter, computer)

or/ee/ist, meaning person (actor, employee, tourist)

Some suffixes change how a word can be used in a sentence or the part of speech. The common grammatical suffixes taught are:

ment, changing part of speech (enjoyment, government)

ness, changing part of speech (kindness, happiness)

tion/sion, changing part of speech (pollution, confusion)

ance, changing part of speech (resistance, performance)

ous, changing part of speech (dangerous, mysterious)

y, changing part of speech (bumpy, sunny)

en, changing part of speech (broken, sadden)

al, changing part of speech (musical, national)

ly, changing part of speech (dangerously, mysteriously)

There are other prefixes and suffixes that occur less frequently. Related words containing these suffixes (**east**, **eastern**; **vary**, **variety**) are included in lessons and sorted for, but these less common suffixes are not the focus of the lesson.

Organizing to Teach Making Words

The materials you need to teach a Making Words lesson are quite simple. You need a pocket chart in which to display the word correctly made with the pocket-chart letters. You need a set of pocket-chart or overhead letters big enough for all the students to see. Also, you need index cards on which to write the words students will make. Most teachers store their index cards for each lesson in an envelope.

Your students need the letters to manipulate. Reproducible letter strips for each lesson are included at the back of this book.

Making Words Homework

Because students like manipulating the letters and coming up with more words than we have time to make in the lesson, a Making Words Take-Home Sheet is a popular activity. You will find a duplicatable template in the back of this book. Write the letters in the boxes at the top in alphabetical order with vowels and then consonants. Students cut or tear the letters apart and fill the boxes with words they can spell with these letters. Encourage them to include words they remember making during the lesson in class and other words they think of.

watermelons

Lesson Focus: **er/est**, meaning more and most
re, meaning back or again

Letters: | a | e | e | o | l | m | n | r | s | t | w |

Make Words: low new seal name/mean east lower newer water
renew rename reseal newest lowest melons
meaner meanest eastern watermelons

Directions: Tell students how many letters to use to make each word.

- Emphasize how changing a few letters or rearranging letters makes different words. Words that can be spelled with the same letters are indicated by a /.

- Give meaning or sentence clues to clarify the word the students are making:

  "Use 4 letters to spell **name**. What is your **name**?"

  "Use the same letters in **name** to spell **mean**. After the argument, the boy was ashamed of the **mean** things he had said."

  "Change the first 2 letters in **lower** to spell **newer**. My car is very old and I am hoping to buy a **newer** one."

  "Use 6 letters to spell **rename**. Sometimes when I am working on the computer I **rename** my document so I can make changes and not lose anything."

- Give the students one minute to figure out the secret word and then give clues if needed.

  "Our secret word is a compound word and we spelled both root words."

Sort Related Words: low, lower, lowest; mean, meaner, meanest; east, eastern; seal, reseal; name, rename; water, melons, watermelons

- Draw students' attention to the words on index cards and have the words pronounced.

- Choose the most complex set of related words and model for students how to use those words in sentences to show how they are related.

  new newer newest renew

  "My husband's car is **newer** than mine but my mom just bought a car and has the **newest** car in the family. I need to **renew** my driver's license before my birthday next month."

  "The suffixes **er** and **est** often mean **more** and **most**. When I **renew** my driver's license, I get a new license back. The prefix **re** sometimes means **back** or **again**."

- Let volunteers choose sets of related words and give sentences that show how words are related. Help them construct sentences and explain prefixes and suffixes as needed.

Transfer Words: reopen, reprint; rich, richer, richest; western, northern

- Have students use sorted words to spell other words. Be sure to have the class decide which related words to use and how to spell the new root word before letting anyone write the word. Talk about spelling changes as needed. Let volunteers use new words in sentences that show meaning.

Lesson 2
grandchildren

Lesson Focus: **er**, meaning person or thing that does something

Letters: | a̲ e̲ i c̲ d̲ d g̲ h̲ l̲ n n̲ r r̲ |

 Make Words: ear race ring/grin grind grand glide ranch dance racer racing glider dancer dancing grinder rancher grinned earring children grandchildren

Directions: Tell students how many letters to use to make each word.

- Emphasize how changing a few letters or rearranging letters makes different words. Words that can be spelled with the same letters are indicated by a /.

- Give meaning or sentence clues to clarify the word the students are making:

    "Use 4 letters to make the word **race**. Who do you think will win the **race**?"

    "Use the same letters in **ring** to spell **grin**. From the **grin** on my cousin's face, I knew he was up to something!"

    "Change the vowel in **grind** to spell **grand**. We had a **grand** time at the circus."

    "Use 7 letters to spell **grinder**. The butcher put the beef into the **grinder** and ground it into hamburger."

- Give the students one minute to figure out the secret word and then give clues if needed.

    "Our secret word is a compound word and we spelled both root words."

 Sort Related Words: dance, dancer, dancing; glide, glider; grind, grinder; ranch, rancher; grin, grinned; ear, ring, earring; grand, children, grandchildren

- Draw students' attention to the words on index cards and have the words pronounced.

- Choose the most complex set of related words and model for students how to use those words in sentences to show how they are related.

    race   racer   racing

    "The one-mile **race** was won by the youngest **racer**. He won the **race** by **racing** past the frontrunner at the very last second."

    "The suffix **er** sometimes means the person who does something. A **racer** is the person who is in the **race**. When we add **ing** to race, we have the word **racing**. When we add **er** or **ing** to a word that ends in **e**, we drop the **e**."

- Let volunteers choose sets of related words and give sentences that show how words are related. Help them construct sentences and explain prefixes and suffixes as needed. Point out spelling changes if your students still need this instruction.

Transfer Words: write, writer, writing; scan, scanner, scanned; jog, jogger, jogging

- Have students use sorted words to spell other words. Be sure to have the class decide which related words to use and how to spell the new root word before letting anyone write the word. Talk about spelling changes as needed. Let volunteers use new words in sentences that show meaning.

Lesson 3
cheerleaders

Lesson Focus: **er**, meaning person or thing that does something
re, meaning back or again

Letters: | a e e e e c d h l r r s |

 Make Words: read   lead/deal   race   racer   cheer   redeal/dealer/leader
reader/reread   search   cheered   searcher/research   cheerleader

Directions: Tell students how many letters to use to make each word.

● Emphasize how changing a few letters or rearranging letters makes different words. Words that can be spelled with the same letters are indicated by a /.

● Give meaning or sentence clues to clarify the word the students are making:

"Use 4 letters to spell the word **read**. I like to **read** books."

"Change the first letter in **read** and you can spell **lead**. Who will **lead** the class in singing that song?"

"Just move the letters around and you can change **lead** to **deal**. I got a great **deal** on my new bike."

"Add a letter to the word **race** to spell **racer**. A person who races is a **racer**."

"Use the same letters in **redeal** to spell **dealer**. The person who passes out the playing cards is the **dealer**."

"Change the letters around again and you have **leader**. The **leader** helped the students answer all the questions on the list."

● Give the students one minute to figure out the secret word and then give clues if needed.

"Our secret word is a compound word and we spelled both root words."

 Sort Related Words: read, reader, reread; lead, leader; deal, dealer, redeal; race, racer; cheer, cheered; search, searcher, research; cheer, leader, cheerleader

● Draw students' attention to the words on index cards and have the words pronounced.

● Choose the most complex set of related words and model for students how to use those words in sentences to show how they are related.

search   searcher   research

"**Search** means to look for something. The suffix **er** sometimes means the person who does something. A **searcher** is a person who searches for something. The prefix **re** means back or again. When we **research** a topic, we search back to find out what was written about it. In fifth grade you will become a **researcher** when you **research** a topic in science."

● Let volunteers choose sets of related words and give sentences that show how words are related. Help them construct sentences and explain prefixes and suffixes as needed.

Transfer Words: reader, reread; builder, rebuild; printer, reprint

- Have students use sorted words to spell other words. Be sure to have the class decide which related words to use and how to spell the new root word before letting anyone write the word. Talk about spelling changes as needed. Let volunteers use new words in sentences that show meaning.

Lesson 4
earthquakes

Lesson Focus: **er**, meaning person or thing that does something
re, meaning back or again

Letters: | a a e e u h k q t r s |

 Make Words: eat use user heat seat take shake quake skate reuse earth eater heater/reheat reseat retake skater shaker earthquakes

Directions: Tell students how many letters to use to make each word.

- Emphasize how changing a few letters or rearranging letters makes different words. Words that can be spelled with the same letters are indicated by a /.

- Give meaning or sentence clues to clarify the word the students are making:

   "Use 3 letters to spell **use**. I will **use** the computer to write my story."

   "Add one letter to **use** and you have the word **user**. A person who uses something is a **user**."

   "Change one letter in **heat** to spell **seat**. Everyone is in their **seat**."

   "Change the letters around in **heater** and you can spell **reheat**. Do you like to **reheat** leftover pizza or eat it cold?"

- Give the students one minute to figure out the secret word and then give clues if needed.

   "Our secret word is a compound word and we spelled both root words."

 Sort Related Words: eat, eater; use, user, reuse; heat, reheat, heater; seat, reseat; take, retake; shake, shaker; skate, skater; earth, quake, earthquakes

- Draw students' attention to the words on index cards and have the words pronounced.

- Choose the most complex set of related words and model for students how to use those words in sentences to show how they are related.

   heat   heater   reheat

   "The suffix **er** sometimes means a thing that does something. A **heater** is a thing that **heats** something. Will you **heat** the new room with that **heater**? When the prefix **re** is added to a word then you do it again. I always **reheat** pizza when I eat it again the next day."

   "A **skater** is the person who **skates**. When we add **er** or **ing** to a word that ends in **e**, we drop the **e** before adding it."

- Let volunteers choose sets of related words and give sentences that show how words are related. Help them construct sentences and explain prefixes and suffixes as needed. Point out spelling changes if your students still need this instruction. Sort related words and use those words in a sentence that shows relationship.

Transfer Words: painter, repaint; opener, reopen; writer, rewrite

- Have students use sorted words to spell other words. Be sure to have the class decide which related words to use and how to spell the new root word before letting anyone write the word. Talk about spelling changes as needed. Let volunteers use new words in sentences that show meaning.

Lesson 5
fingerprints

Lesson Focus: **er/est**, meaning more and most
er, meaning person or thing that does something
re, meaning back or again

Letters: <u>e</u> <u>i</u> <u>i</u> <u>f</u> <u>g</u> <u>n</u> <u>n</u> <u>p</u> <u>r</u> <u>r</u> <u>s</u> <u>t</u>

 Make Words: tip spin sift fine sting print finer finest sprint
sifter finger spinner stinger printer/reprint sprinter
fingertips fingerprints

Directions: Tell students how many letters to use to make each word.

- Emphasize how changing a few letters or rearranging letters makes different words. Words that can be spelled with the same letters are indicated by a /.

- Give meaning or sentence clues to clarify the word the students are making:

    "Use 3 letters to spell **tip**. I **tip** the container to try to get the last of the drink."

    "Use 4 letters and spell the word **spin**. Try not to **spin** around."

    "Use 6 letters and spell the word **sifter**. We sift flour in a flour **sifter**."

    "Change the letters around in **printer** and you can spell **reprint**. Did you **reprint** after you found your mistakes?"

- Give the students one minute to figure out the secret word and then give clues if needed.

    "Our secret word is a compound word and we spelled both root words."

 Sort Related Words: spin, spinner; sift, sifter; sting, stinger; sprint, sprinter; print, printer, reprint; fine, finer, finest; tip, finger, fingertips; print, finger, fingerprints

- Draw students' attention to the words on index cards and have the words pronounced.

- Choose the most complex set of related words and model for students how to use those words in sentences to show how they are related.

    print printer reprint

    "The suffix **er** sometimes means a person or thing that does something. A **printer** is a thing that **prints** something. We use a **printer** to **print** our stories and reports. When the prefix **re** is added to a word then you do it again. We always **reprint** a story if we find a mistake or need another copy."

    "A **spinner** is the person who **spins**. Sometimes we have to double the consonant at the end of a word before we add **er**, like in **spinner**."

- Let volunteers choose sets of related words and give sentences that show how words are related. Help them construct sentences and explain prefixes and suffixes as needed. Point out spelling changes if your students still need this instruction.

Transfer Words: play, player, replay; drum, drummer; nice, nicer, nicest

- Have students use sorted words to spell other words. Be sure to have the class decide which related words to use and how to spell the new root word before letting anyone write the word. Talk about spelling changes as needed. Let volunteers use new words in sentences that show meaning.

Lesson 6
quarterbacks

Lesson Focus: **er**, meaning person or thing that does something

Letters: | a | a | e | u | b | c | k | q | r | r | s | t |

 Make Words: set seat rest back bake baker truck track trace skate skater tracer backer tracker trucker quarter setback backrest backseat quarterbacks

Directions: Tell students how many letters to use to make each word.

- Emphasize how changing a few letters or rearranging letters makes different words.

- Give meaning or sentence clues to clarify the word the students are making:

    "Use 3 letters to spell **set**. I **set** the table each night for our dinner."

    "Add one letter to spell the word **seat**. Your **seat** is where you sit."

    "Add a letter to **bake** and you have **baker**. I am the cake **baker** in my family."

    "Change the vowel in **tracker** and you can spell **trucker**. If you drive a truck you are a **trucker**."

- Give the students one minute to figure out the secret word and then give clues if needed.

    "Our secret word is a compound word and we spelled both root words."

 Sort Related Words: back, backer; bake, baker; truck, trucker; track, tracker; trace, tracer; skate, skater; back, set, setback; back, rest, backrest; back, seat, backseat; quarter, back, quarterbacks

- Draw students' attention to the words on index cards and have the words pronounced.

- Choose one set of related words and model for students how to use those words in sentences to show how they are related.

    track   tracker

    "The suffix **er** sometimes means a person or thing that does something. A **tracker** is a person who **tracks** something. The police sometimes use a person with a dog that can **track** as their **tracker** when someone is missing."

    "A compound word is made up of two words. The word **set** and **back** make the compound word **setback**. I had a **setback** to finishing my research paper when my computer broke down."

    "A **baker** is the person who **bakes**. Sometimes we have to drop the **e** at the end of a word before we add **er** like in **baker**."

- Let volunteers choose sets of related words and give sentences that show how words are related. Help them construct sentences and explain prefixes and suffixes as needed. Point out spelling changes if your students still need this instruction.

Transfer Words: stack, stacker; pace, pacer; full, back, fullback

- Have students use sorted words to spell other words. Be sure to have the class decide which related words to use and how to spell the new root word before letting anyone write the word. Talk about spelling changes as needed. Let volunteers use new words in sentences that show meaning.

Lesson 7

searchlight

Lesson Focus: **er/est**, meaning more and most
ist, meaning person

Letters: a e i c g h h l r s t

 Make Words: rich   real   race   high   large   light   eight   eighth   search
ethics   racist   higher   highest   richest   largest   realist
ethical   lightest   searchlight

Directions: Tell students how many letters to use to make each word.

- Emphasize how changing a few letters or rearranging letters makes different words.

- Give meaning or sentence clues to clarify the word the students are making:

  "Use 4 letters to spell **rich**. If you have lots of money you might be **rich**."

  "Change one letter in **light** to spell the word **eight**. Do you remember when you were **eight?**"

  "Add a letter to **eight** and you have **eighth**. Who is the **eighth** one in line?"

  "You have made the word **higher**; now make the word **highest**. Who got the **highest** score?"

  "Use 7 letters and spell the word **ethical**. If you are **ethical**, you don't lie or cheat."

- Give the students one minute to figure out the secret word and then give clues if needed.

  "Our secret word is a compound word and we spelled both root words."

 Sort Related Words: high, higher, highest; rich, richest; large, largest; light, lightest; eight, eighth; race, racist; real, realist; ethics, ethical; search, light, searchlight

- Draw students' attention to the words on index cards and have the words pronounced.

- Choose one set of related words and model for students how to use those words in sentences to show how they are related.

  high   higher   highest

  "The suffix **er** sometimes means **more**. A building can be **high** but a **higher** building is more high. The suffix **est** sometimes means the **most**. The **highest** building is the most high of all the buildings."

  "A compound word is made up of two words. The word **search** and **light** make up the compound word **searchlight**. The **searchlight** was at the top of the lighthouse."

  "A **racist** is a person who is aware of everyone's **race**. Sometimes we have to drop the **e** at the end of a word before we add **ist** like in **racist**."

- Let volunteers choose sets of related words and give sentences that show how words are related. Help them construct sentences and explain prefixes and suffixes as needed. Point out spelling changes if needed.

Transfer Words: poor, poorer, poorest; smart, smarter, smartest; artist, activist

- Have students use sorted words to spell other words. Be sure to have the class decide which related words to use and how to spell the new root word before letting anyone write the word. Talk about spelling changes as needed. Let volunteers use new words in sentences that show meaning.

Lesson 8
planetarium

Lesson Focus: **un**, meaning not or opposite
im, meaning in
re, meaning back or again
er, meaning person or thing that does something

Letters: a a e i u l m n p r t

 Make Words: real ripe mine time timer miner ripen paint plant planet unreal unripe planter/replant implant painter/repaint planetarium

Directions: Tell students how many letters to use to make each word.

- Emphasize how changing a few letters or rearranging letters makes different words. Words that can be spelled with the same letters are indicated by a /.

- Give meaning or sentence clues to clarify the word the students are making:

  "Use 4 letters to make the word **real**. The creatures in the movie were animated but they looked very **real**."

  "Use 6 letters to spell the word **unreal**. Everyone said that watching the tornado touch down felt very **unreal**."

  "Change the first 2 letters in **replant** to spell **implant**. If your heart does not have a steady beat, doctors can **implant** a pacemaker into your body to regulate your heartbeat."

  "Use the same letters in **planter** to spell **replant**. Every year I **replant** the shrubs that die over the winter."

- Give the students one minute to figure out the secret word and then give clues if needed.

  "Our secret word today is related to the word **planet**. Start with the word **planet** and add your other letters to it."

 Sort Related Words: real, unreal; ripe, unripe, ripen; mine, miner; time, timer; paint, painter, repaint; plant, planter, replant, implant; planet, planetarium

- Draw students' attention to the words on index cards and have the words pronounced.

- Choose the most complex of the related words and model for students how to use those words in sentences to show how they are related.

  plant planter replant implant

  "A **planter** is a container you plant things in. When you **replant** something, you **plant** it again. When you **implant** something, you plant it in something or somebody. The **er** suffix can be a person or a thing. **Re** is a prefix that sometimes means again. **Im** is a prefix that sometimes means in."

- Let volunteers choose sets of related words and help them construct sentences and explain how the prefixes and suffixes change the root words. "A **planetarium** is a place. Other place words that end in **ium** are **stadium**, **gymnasium**, **aquarium**, **terrarium**, and **auditorium**."

Transfer Words: unfair, unpainted; rebuild, refill; leader, driver

- Have students use sorted words to spell other words. Be sure to have the class decide which related words to use and how to spell the new root word before letting anyone write the word. Let volunteers use new words in sentences that show meaning.

Lesson 9

unfriendly

Lesson Focus: **un**, meaning not or opposite
re, meaning back or again
ly, changing part of speech
y, changing part of speech

Letters: | e | i | u | d | f | l | n | n | r | y |

 Make Words: in   run   fun   fund   rude   line   dine   diner   funny   runny   inner   unify   friend   rudely   refund   reunify   unlined   friendly   unfriendly

Directions: Tell students how many letters to use to make each word.

- Emphasize how changing a few letters or rearranging letters makes different words.

- Give meaning or sentence clues to clarify the word the students are making:

  "Use 3 letters to make the word **run**. I like to **run** around the track after school."

  "Change a letter in **run** to spell the word **fun**. It is **fun** to play soccer."

  "Add a letter to **fun** and you can spell **fund**. The money was put in a special **fund**."

  "Use 5 letters to spell the word **funny**. Everyone said the movie was **funny**."

  "Change the first letter in **funny** to spell **runny**. The worst thing about a cold is the **runny** nose."

  "Use 7 letters to spell **reunify**. We will try to **reunify** our group."

- Give the students one minute to figure out the secret word and then give clues if needed.

  "Our secret word today is related to the word **friend** with a prefix and suffix added."

 Sort Related Words: **in, inner; run, runny; fun, funny; line, unlined; fund, refund; unify, reunify; dine, diner; rude, rudely; friend, friendly, unfriendly**

- Draw students' attention to the words on index cards and have the words pronounced.

- Choose the most complex of the related words and model for students how to use those words in sentences to show how they are related.

  friend   friendly   unfriendly

  "A **friend** is someone you really like. To be **friendly** is to be nice to someone. When someone is **unfriendly** he or she is not very nice to you. The prefix **un** often changes a word to the opposite meaning."

- Let volunteers choose sets of related words and help them construct sentences and explain how the prefixes and suffixes change the root words.

Transfer Words: unlucky, unkind; reclaim, resend; sunny, skinny; madly, timely

- Have students use sorted words to spell other words. Be sure to have the class decide which related words to use and how to spell the new root word before letting anyone write the word. Let volunteers use new words in sentences that show meaning.

Lesson 10
unfriendliest

Lesson Focus: **un**, meaning not or opposite
under, meaning under or less
re, meaning back or again
er, meaning person or thing that does something

Letters: e e i i u d f l n n r s t

 Make Words: fund   fuel   rude   line   send   lend   dine   diner   unite
friend   sender   lender   rudely   refund   refuel   reunite
unlined   underline   friendliest   unfriendliest

Directions: Tell students how many letters to use to make each word.

- Emphasize how changing a few letters or rearranging letters makes different words.

- Give meaning or sentence clues to clarify the word the students are making:

   "Use 4 letters to make the word **fund**. I put my money in a money market **fund** at the bank."

   "Change a letter in the word **send** to spell **lend**. I will **lend** you some money."

   "Add a letter to **dine** and spell **diner**. Do you like to eat at the **diner?**"

   "Change the first letter in **sender** and you can spell **lender**. A person who lends money is a **lender**."

   "You have spelled **fund**; now spell **refund**. I received my tax **refund**."

- Give the students one minute to figure out the secret word and then give clues if needed.

   "Our secret word today is again related to the word **friend**."

 Sort Related Words: fund, refund; fuel, refuel; unite, reunite; send, sender;
lend, lender; dine, diner; line, unlined, underline;
rude, rudely; friend, friendliest, unfriendliest

- Draw students' attention to the words on index cards and have the words pronounced.

- Choose a set of related words and model for students how to use those words in sentences to show how they are related.

   line   unlined   underlined

   "A **line** is a straight mark between two places. If paper does not have lines it is **unlined**. When a line is under a word it is **underlined**. The prefix **un** turns the word **lined** into the opposite meaning, **unlined**. **Under** is a prefix that sometimes means under."

- Let volunteers choose sets of related words and help them construct sentences and explain how the prefixes and suffixes change the root words.

Transfer Words: resend, reappear; unkind, unlucky;
underground, underwear, underwater

- Have students use sorted words to spell other words. Be sure to have the class decide which related words to use and how to spell the new root word before letting anyone write the word. Let volunteers use new words in sentences that show meaning.

Lesson 11
unfriendliness

Lesson Focus: **un**, meaning not or opposite
under, meaning under or less
re, meaning back or again
less, meaning less or without
ness, changing part of speech

Letters: e e i i u d f l n n r s s

Make Words: red end use rude fund fuel line under reuse
refund refuel friend endless redness rudeness
underline friendless friendliness unfriendliness

Directions: Tell students how many letters to use to make each word.

● Emphasize how changing a few letters or rearranging letters makes different words.

● Give meaning or sentence clues to clarify the word the students are making:

"Use 4 letters to make the word **rude**. Nobody likes people who are **rude** and impolite."

"Use 7 letters to spell **redness**. The nurse was worried about the **redness** around the gash on the patient's arm."

"Use 12 letters to spell **friendliness**. The **friendliness** in the room was felt by all the students."

● Give the students one minute to figure out the secret word and then give clues if needed.

"Our secret word today is the opposite of **friendliness**."

Sort Related Words: use, reuse; fund, refund; fuel, refuel; red, redness;
rude, rudeness; line, under, underline; end, endless;
friend, friendless, friendliness, unfriendliness

● Draw students' attention to the words on index cards and have the words pronounced.

● Choose a set of related words and model for students how to use those words in sentences to show how they are related.

rude rudeness

"The clerk was very **rude** to the customers and he was later fired for his **rudeness**. **Ness** is a suffix we add to words to change how that word is used in a sentence."

● Let volunteers choose sets of related words and help them construct sentences and explain how the prefixes and suffixes change the root words.

Transfer Words: unhappy, happiness; unfair, fairness; unkind, kindness

● Have students use sorted words to spell other words. Be sure to have the class decide which related words to use and how to spell the new root word before letting anyone write the word. Remind the students that they must change the **y** to **i** before adding **ness** in **happiness**—just like in **friendliness**. Let volunteers use new words in sentences that show meaning.

Lesson 12

personality

Lesson Focus: **er/ist**, meaning person or thing that does something
re, meaning back or again
ly, changing part of speech

Letters: a e i o l n p r s t y

 Make Words: play part easy paint plant panel partly easily
person staple replay/player repaint/painter replant/planter
stapler panelist personal personality

Directions: Tell students how many letters to use to make each word.

- Emphasize how changing a few letters or rearranging letters makes different words. Words that can be spelled with the same letters are indicated by a /.

- Give meaning or sentence clues to clarify the word the students are making:

    "Use 5 letters to make the word **paint**. I like to **paint** but I have to be careful."

    "You have made the word **replay**; now move the letters around and spell **player**. She is the best **player** on the team."

    "Use 8 letters to spell the word **panelist**. I was asked to be a **panelist** and sit in front of the students and answer the questions."

- Give the students one minute to figure out the secret word and then give clues if needed.

    "Our secret word today is related to the word **person**."

 Sort Related Words: play, player, replay; paint, painter, repaint;
plant, replant, planter; easy, easily; part, partly;
staple, stapler; panel, panelist;
person, personal, personality

- Draw students' attention to the words on index cards and have the words pronounced.

- Choose a set of related words and model for students how to use those words in sentences to show how they are related.

    panelist panel

    "A **panelist** is a member of a **panel**. The suffix **ist** often means a person who does something, as in the words **artist**, **scientist**, and **tourist**."

- Let volunteers choose sets of related words and help them construct sentences and explain how the prefixes and suffixes change the root words.

Transfer Words: artist, tourist, cyclist, colonist; nearly, busily, happily

- Have students use sorted words to spell other words. Be sure to have the class decide which related words to use and how to spell the new root word before letting anyone write the word. Remind the students that they must change the **y** to **i** before adding **ly** in **busily** and **happily**—just like in **easily**. Let volunteers use new words in sentences that show meaning.

Lesson 13
carelessly

Lesson Focus: **less**, meaning less or without
ly, changing part of speech
y, changing part of speech
re, meaning back or again

Letters: | a | e | e | c | l | l | r | s | s | y |

 Make Words: call   care   real   seal/sale   scale   scare   scary   scaly
class   clear   recall/caller   resale/reseal   classy   really
clearly   careless   carelessly

Directions: Tell students how many letters to use to make each word.

- Emphasize how changing a few letters or rearranging letters makes different words. Words that can be spelled with the same letters are indicated by a /.

- Give meaning or sentence clues to clarify the word the students are making:

  "Change a letter in **real** to spell the word **seal**. The letter had a **seal** on the envelope."

  "Change the letters around in **seal** to spell the word **sale**. It is fun to buy things you want when they are on **sale**."

  "Add a letter to **sale** and you can spell the word **scale**. **Scale** can mean something you use to weigh something or the covering on a fish's body."

  "Change the letters around in **resale** and you can spell **reseal**. You need to **reseal** the envelope before you mail it."

- Give the students one minute to figure out the secret word and then give clues if needed.

  "Our secret word today is related to the word **careless**."

 Sort Related Words: call, caller, recall; seal, reseal; sale, resale; scale, scaly;
scare, scary; class, classy; real, really; clear, clearly;
care, careless, carelessly

- Draw students' attention to the words on index cards and have the words pronounced.

- Choose a set of related words and model for students how to use those words in sentences to show how they are related.

  "A fish has **scales** covering its body and we say fish are **scaly**. **Y** is a suffix that changes how a word can be used in a sentence."

- Let volunteers choose sets of related words and help them construct sentences and explain how the prefixes and suffixes change the root words.

Transfer Words: smelly, juicy, crabby; **useless, helpless, harmless**

- Have students use sorted words to spell other words. Be sure to have the class decide which related words to use and how to spell the new root word before letting anyone write the word. Point out spelling changes. Let volunteers use new words in sentences that show meaning.

Lesson 14
meaningless

Lesson Focus: **less**, meaning less or without
ness, changing part of speech

Letters: a e e i g l m n n s s

 Make Words: man age aim less mile mean/name lame sales
ageless aimless mileage meaning nameless lameness
salesman meaningless

Directions: Tell students how many letters to use to make each word.

- Emphasize how changing a few letters or rearranging letters makes different words. Words that can be spelled with the same letters are indicated by a /.

- Give meaning or sentence clues to clarify the word the students are making:

    "Use 4 letters to make the word **mean**. What do you **mean**?"

    "Change the letters around in **mean** to spell the word **name**. What is his **name**?"

    "Change one letter in **name** and spell **lame**. When a dog cannot walk right we say it is **lame**."

    "Use 8 letters and make **nameless**. Many speech writers are **nameless** to the public."

    "Use 8 letters and spell **salesman**. A person who sells things is a **salesman**."

- Give the students one minute to figure out the secret word and then give clues if needed.

    "Our secret word today is related to the word **meaning**."

 Sort Related Words: age, ageless; aim, aimless; name, nameless;
mean, meaning, meaningless; mile, mileage;
lame, lameness; man, sales, salesman

- Draw students' attention to the words on index cards and have the words pronounced.

- Choose a set of related words and model for students how to use those words in sentences to show how they are related.

    "No one knew the man's **age** but everyone agreed the man was **ageless**. He never seemed to get any older. **Less** is a suffix that means less or without."

- Let volunteers choose sets of related words and help them construct sentences and explain how the prefixes and suffixes change the root words.

Transfer Words: endless, fearless, homeless, priceless, painless; hopeless, hopelessness

- Have students use sorted words to spell other words. Be sure to have the class decide which related words to use and how to spell the new root word before letting anyone write the word. Let volunteers use new words in sentences that show meaning.

Lesson 15
mercilessly

Lesson Focus: **er**, meaning person or thing that does something
re, meaning back or again
less, meaning less or without
ly, changing part of speech
y, changing part of speech

Letters: <u>e</u> <u>e</u> <u>i</u> <u>c</u> <u>l</u> <u>l</u> <u>m</u> <u>r</u> <u>s</u> <u>s</u> <u>y</u>

 Make Words: cry   sell   mess   messy   mercy   cries   miser   slice
slime   slimy   smell   smelly   slicer   seller/resell   messily
miserly   merciless   mercilessly

Directions: Tell students how many letters to use to make each word.

- Emphasize how changing a few letters or rearranging letters makes different words. Words that can be spelled with the same letters are indicated by a /.

- Give meaning or sentence clues to clarify the word the students are making:

    "Add a letter to **mess** and you have **messy**. He tried not to be **messy** when making his lunch."

    "Change a letters in **slice** and you can make the word **slime**. The mud on the bottom of the lake felt like **slime**."

    "Use the same letters in **seller** to spell **resell**. Some people buy old houses, fix them up, and **resell** them."

    "Use 7 letters and spell **miserly**. He did not like to spend any money and people said he was **miserly**."

- Give the students one minute to figure out the secret word and then give clues if needed.

    "Our secret word today is related to the word **mercy**."

 Sort Related Words: sell, seller, resell; slice, slicer; cry, cries; slime, slimy;
smell, smelly; mess, messy, messily; miser, miserly;
mercy, merciless, mercilessly

- Draw students' attention to the words on index cards and have the words pronounced.

- Choose a set of related words and model for students how to use those words in sentences to show how they are related.

    "If you make a **mess**, people might say you are **messy** or that you worked **messily**. **Y** and **ly** are suffixes that change how words can be used in sentences."

- Let volunteers choose sets of related words and help them construct sentences and explain how the prefixes and suffixes change the root words.

Transfer Words: lucky, luckily; sleepy, sleepily, sleepless; hopeless, hopelessly

- Have students use sorted words to spell other words. Be sure to have the class decide which related words to use and how to spell the new root word before letting anyone write the word. If needed, remind the students that they have to change the **y** to **i** when adding **ly**. Let volunteers use new words in sentences that show meaning.

Lesson 16
gracefully

Lesson Focus: **ful**, meaning full or with
re, meaning back or again
ly, changing part of speech
y, changing part of speech

Letters: | a̲ e̲ u̲ c̲ f̲ g̲ l̲ l̲ r̲ y̲ |

 Make Words: care curl real call full fully curly cruel clear large caller/recall really cruelly clearly largely careful graceful carefully gracefully

Directions: Tell students how many letters to use to make each word.

- Emphasize how changing a few letters or rearranging letters makes different words. Words that can be spelled with the same letters are indicated by a /.

- Give meaning or sentence clues to clarify the word the students are making:

    "Add a letter to **full** and you can spell **fully**. When you are **fully** satisfied, you don't want more to eat."

    "Use the same letters in **caller** and you can spell **recall**. When I finish calling all the people on the team, I will **recall** those I did not get to talk to."

    "Use 9 letters and spell **carefully**. He worked **carefully** on his math test."

- Give the students one minute to figure out the secret word and then give clues if needed.

    "Our secret word today is related to the word **grace**."

 Sort Related Words: **curl, curly; full, fully; clear, clearly; real, really; large, largely; cruel, cruelly; call, recall, caller; care, careful, carefully; graceful, gracefully**

- Draw students' attention to the words on index cards and have the words pronounced.

- Choose a set of related words and model for students how to use those words in sentences to show how they are related.

    "If you use **care** you are **careful** and you try to do things **carefully** at all times. The suffix **ful** means full of or with. The suffix **ly** changes how a word can be used in a sentence."

- Let volunteers choose sets of related words and help them construct sentences and explain how the prefixes and suffixes change the root words.

 Transfer Words: **hopeful, hopefully; cheerful, cheerfully; peaceful, peacefully; grateful, gratefully**

- Have students use sorted words to spell other words. Be sure to have the class decide which related words to use and how to spell the new root word before letting anyone write the word. Let volunteers use new words in sentences that show meaning.

Lesson 17
unfortunately

Lesson Focus: **un**, meaning not or opposite
en, changing part of speech
ly, changing part of speech

Letters: | a e o u u f l n n r t t y |

Make Words: ran rot fat flat real true truly untrue unreal
outran rotten fatten fatter flatter flatten fortune
fortunate fortunately unfortunate unfortunately

Directions: Tell students how many letters to use to make each word.

- Emphasize how changing a few letters or rearranging letters makes different words.

- Give meaning or sentence clues to clarify the word the students are making:

    "Add a letter to **fat** and you can spell **flat**. I had to wait for the service truck to come and fix my **flat** tire."

    "Use 5 letters and make the word **truly**. I was **truly** sorry that I made a mistake."

    "Add a letter to **fatter** and spell **flatter**. My design was **flatter** on the top."

    "Add 2 letters to **fortunate** and spell **fortunately**. **Fortunately** I was prepared for the test."

- Give the students one minute to figure out the secret word and then give clues if needed.

    "Our secret word today is related to the word **fortunate**."

Sort Related Words: fat, fatter, fatten; flat, flatter, flatten; rot, rotten;
true, truly, untrue; real, unreal; ran, outran;
fortune, fortunate, fortunately, unfortunate, unfortunately

- Draw students' attention to the words on index cards and have the words pronounced.

- Choose a set of related words and model for students how to use those words in sentences to show how they are related.

    "Our dog was **fat** before he got sick and lost a lot of weight. We fed him his special dog food to **fatten** him up and in a few weeks he was much **fatter**. **En** is a suffix that changes how a word can be used in a sentence. The suffix **er** often means more."

- Let volunteers choose sets of related words and help them construct sentences and explain how the prefixes and suffixes change the root words.

Transfer Words: written, unwritten; broken, unbroken;
tighten, tightly; beaten, unbeaten

- Have students use sorted words to spell other words. Be sure to have the class decide which related words to use and how to spell the new root word before letting anyone write the word. Let volunteers use new words in sentences that show meaning.

Lesson 18
unworkable

Lesson Focus: **able**, meaning able to
un, meaning not or opposite
er, meaning person or thing that does something
en, changing part of speech

Letters: a e o u b k l n r w

 Make Words: own able real bake bank walk work woke woken
owner baker broke broken banker walker unable
unreal workable unworkable

Directions: Tell students how many letters to use to make each word.

- Emphasize how changing a few letters or rearranging letters makes different words.

- Give meaning or sentence clues to clarify the word the students are making:

    "Add a letter to the word **woke** and you can spell **woken**. I was **woken** up by the noise I heard outside."

    "Add a letter to **broke** and spell **broken**. My new vase got **broken** when it fell off the shelf."

    "Use 8 letters to spell **workable**. I was very busy and a boy in my neighborhood needed cash. I paid him to mow my lawn and this was a **workable** solution to both our problems."

- Give the students one minute to figure out the secret word and then give clues if needed.

    "Our secret word today is related to the word **work**."

 Sort Related Words: **own, owner; bake, baker; bank, banker; walk, walker; woke, woken; broke, broken; real, unreal; able, unable; work, workable, unworkable**

- Draw students' attention to the words on index cards and have the words pronounced.

- Choose a set of related words and model for students how to use those words in sentences to show how they are related.

    "If something **works**, it is a good solution. If something is **workable** you can do it or solve it. If it is **unworkable** you can't! **Able** is a suffix that means able to. **Un** is a prefix that changes a word to the opposite meaning."

- Let volunteers choose sets of related words and help them construct sentences and explain how the prefixes and suffixes change the root words.

 Transfer Words: **washable, unwashable; lovable, unlovable; favorable, unfavorable**

- Have students use sorted words to spell other words. Be sure to have the class decide which related words to use and how to spell the new root word before letting anyone write the word. Let volunteers use new words in sentences that show meaning.

Lesson 19
unbreakable

Lesson Focus: **un**, meaning not or opposite
en, meaning to make
able, meaning able to
er, meaning person or thing that does something

Letters: | a | a | e | e | u | b | b | k | l | n | r |

Make Words: burn   bear   real   able   bank   bake   baker/break
banker   unreal   unable   enable   burnable   bearable
breakable   unbearable   unbreakable

Directions: Tell students how many letters to use to make each word.

- Emphasize how changing a few letters or rearranging letters makes different words. Words that can be spelled with the same letters are indicated by a /.

- Give meaning or sentence clues to clarify the word the students are making:

    "Move the letters around and **baker** becomes **break**. Did you ever **break** your arm or leg?"

    "Change a letter in **unable** and spell **enable**. The new tires will **enable** the race car driver to win."

    "Use 8 letters to spell **burnable**. Newspaper is very **burnable**."

    "Use 9 letters to spell **breakable**. My new glasses are **breakable**."

- Give the students one minute to figure out the secret word and then give clues if needed.

    "Our secret word today is related to the word **break**."

Sort Related Words: bake, baker; bank, banker; real, unreal; able, unable, enable;
burn, burnable; bear, bearable, unbearable;
break, breakable, unbreakable

- Draw students' attention to the words on index cards and have the words pronounced.

- Choose a set of related words and model for students how to use those words in sentences to show how they are related.

    "If the pain is **bearable** you can **bear** it. If it is **unbearable** you cannot. **Able** is a suffix that means able to. **Un** is a prefix that changes a word to the opposite meaning."

- Let volunteers choose sets of related words and help them construct sentences and explain how the prefixes and suffixes change the root words.

Transfer Words: driver, drivable, undrivable; livable, unlivable;
worker, workable, unworkable

- Have students use sorted words to spell other words. Be sure to have the class decide which related words to use and how to spell the new root word before letting anyone write the word. Let volunteers use new words in sentences that show meaning.

41

Lesson 20
undesirable

Lesson Focus: **un**, meaning not or opposite
dis, meaning not or opposite
en, meaning to make
re, meaning back or again
able, meaning able to
er, meaning person or thing that does

Letters: a e e i u b d l n r s

 Make Words: use able dear sure build blend reuse usable unable enable ensure endear desire disable blender builder/rebuild reusable desirable undesirable

Directions: Tell students how many letters to use to make each word.

- Emphasize how changing a few letters or rearranging letters makes different words. Words that can be spelled with the same letters are indicated by a /.

- Give meaning or sentence clues to clarify the word the students are making:

    "Change one letter in **usable** to spell **unable**. He is **unable** to make that word."

    "Change a letter in **unable** and spell **enable**. Studying will **enable** me to do well on the test."

    "Move 2 letters around in **builder** and spell **rebuild**. Who can **rebuild** the house after the storm?"

- Give the students one minute to figure out the secret word and then give clues if needed.

    "Our secret word today is related to the word **desire**."

 Sort Related Words: use, usable, reuse, reusable; able, enable, unable, disable; dear, endear; sure, ensure; blend, blender; build, builder, rebuild; desire, desirable, undesirable

- Draw students' attention to the words on index cards and have the words pronounced.

- Choose a set of related words and model for students how to use those words in sentences to show how they are related.

    "When you make someone able to do something, you **enable** them to do it. When someone is not able to do something, we say they are **unable**. When you make something unable to work, you **disable** it. The prefix **en** sometimes means to make. The prefixes **un** and **dis** change words to their opposite meanings."

- Let volunteers choose sets of related words and help them construct sentences and explain how the prefixes and suffixes change the root words.

Transfer Words: enact, ensure, endanger; dislike, disprove, disagree

- Have students use sorted words to spell other words. Be sure to have the class decide which related words to use and how to spell the new root word before letting anyone write the word. Let volunteers use new words in sentences that show meaning.

Lesson 21
questionable

Lesson Focus: **un**, meaning not or opposite
en, meaning to make
able, meaning able to
tion, changing part of speech

Letters: | a e e i o u b l n q s t |

 Make Words: tie   seal   suit   able   note   quote   quest   equal
untie   unseal   unable   enable   stable   notable   quotable
suitable   equation   unstable   question   questionable

Directions: Tell students how many letters to use to make each word.

- Emphasize how changing a few letters or rearranging letters makes different words.

- Give meaning or sentence clues to clarify the word the students are making:

    "Use 4 letters to make the word **note**. Did you ever write a thank you **note**?"

    "Use 5 letters to spell **quote**. You have to put quotation marks around a **quote**."

    "Change one letter in **unable** to spell **enable**. The new computer will **enable** her to look up information on the Internet."

    "Change 2 letters in **enable** and spell **stable**. After the accident, the doctor said the patient's condition was **stable**."

    "Use 8 letters to spell **suitable**. The land was **suitable** for building."

- Give the students one minute to figure out the secret word and then give clues if needed.

    "Our secret word today is related to the word **question**."

 Sort Related Words: tie, untie; seal, unseal; able, enable, unable; stable, unstable; note, notable; quote, quotable; suit, suitable; equal, equation; quest, question, questionable

- Draw students' attention to the words on index cards and have the words pronounced.

- Choose a set of related words and model for students how to use those words in sentences to show how they are related.

    "A **quest** is a search. A **question** is when you ask or search for an answer. When something is **questionable** it means you question it. The suffix **tion** changes how a word can be used in a sentence. The suffix **able** means able to."

- Let volunteers choose sets of related words and help them construct sentences and explain how the prefixes and suffixes change the root words.

Transfer Words: solve, solvable, unsolvable; quotation;
rotate, rotation; locate, location

- Have students use sorted words to spell other words. Be sure to have the class decide which related words to use and how to spell the new root word before letting anyone write the word. Let volunteers use new words in sentences that show meaning.

Lesson 22

unpredictable

Lesson Focus: **un**, meaning not or opposite
re, meaning back or again
in, meaning not or opposite
able, meaning able to

Letters: a e e i u b c d l n p r t

 Make Words: cure   paid   tied   build   place   paint   plant   repaid
unpaid   untied   predict   builder/rebuild   replaced   repainted
replanted   incurable   predictable   unpredictable

Directions: Tell students how many letters to use to make each word.

- Emphasize how changing a few letters or rearranging letters makes different words. Words that can be spelled with the same letters are indicated by a /.

- Give meaning or sentence clues to clarify the word the students are making:

   "Use 4 letters to make the word **cure**. Did the medicine **cure** your cold?"

   "Use 6 letters and spell **repaid**. I **repaid** the money I owed."

   "Change 2 letters in **repaid** and make **unpaid**. Something that is not paid is **unpaid**."

   "Use the same letters in **builder** and you can spell **rebuild**."

   "Use 9 letters to spell **incurable**. Some diseases can be cured but others are **incurable**."

- Give the students one minute to figure out the secret word and then give clues if needed.

   "Our secret word today is related to the word **predict**."

 Sort Related Words: tied, untied; **paid, unpaid, repaid; build, builder, rebuild;**
place, replaced; plant, replanted; paint, repainted;
cure, incurable; predict, predictable, unpredictable

- Draw students' attention to the words on index cards and have the words pronounced.

- Choose a set of related words and model for students how to use those words in sentences to show how they are related.

   "Doctors have found many ways to **cure** diseases today that 50 years ago were **incurable**. **Able** is a suffix meaning able. **In** changes a word to its opposite meaning."

- Let volunteers choose sets of related words and help them construct sentences and explain how the prefixes and suffixes change the root words.

Transfer Words: correct, incorrect; complete, incomplete; dependent, independent

- Have students use sorted words to spell other words. Be sure to have the class decide which related words to use and how to spell the new root word before letting anyone write the word. Let volunteers use new words in sentences that show meaning.

Lesson 23

uncomfortable

Lesson Focus: **un**, meaning not or opposite
re, meaning back or again
ful, meaning full or with
able, meaning able to

Letters: | a | e | o | o | u | b | c | f | l | m | n | r | t |

 Make Words: arm room care cure able real count clear
unreal unable armful careful roomful recount
unclear curable comfort countable comfortable
uncomfortable

Directions: Tell students how many letters to use to make each word.

- Emphasize how changing a few letters or rearranging letters makes different words.

- Give meaning or sentence clues to clarify the word the students are making:

  "Change 1 letter in **care** and spell **cure**. Will taking a pill **cure** you?"

  "Use 9 letters to spell **countable**. If you are able to count something it is **countable**."

  "Use 11 letters and make the word **comfortable**. This couch is very **comfortable**."

- Give the students one minute to figure out the secret word and then give clues if needed.

  "Our secret word today is related to the word **comfort**."

 Sort Related Words: arm, armful; care, careful; room, roomful; real, unreal;
clear, unclear; able, unable; cure, curable; count, recount,
countable; comfort, comfortable, uncomfortable

- Draw students' attention to the words on index cards and have the words pronounced.

- Choose a set of related words and model for students how to use those words in sentences to show how they are related.

  "It the election results are close, officials may **recount** the ballots. Anything you can **count** is **countable**. The prefix **re** means back or again. The suffix **able** means able to."

- Let volunteers choose sets of related words and help them construct sentences and explain how the prefixes and suffixes change the root words.

 Transfer Words: handful, houseful, spoonful; suitable, unsuitable;
favorable, unfavorable

- Have students use sorted words to spell other words. Be sure to have the class decide which related words to use and how to spell the new root word before letting anyone write the word. Let volunteers use new words in sentences that show meaning.

Lesson 24

undependable

Lesson Focus: **un**, meaning not or opposite
able, meaning able to
re, meaning back or again
en, meaning to make

Letters: a e e e u b d d l n n p

 Make Words: bend   need   lead   able   plane   unbend   unable   enable
depend   bundle   bundled   deplane   unleaded   unneeded
dependable   undependable

Directions: Tell students how many letters to use to make each word.

● Emphasize how changing a few letters or rearranging letters makes different words.

● Give meaning or sentence clues to clarify the word the students are making:

"Use 4 letters to spell **lead**. The **lead** in your pencil is what makes a mark."

"Change one letter and **unable** becomes **enable**. If you **enable** someone you allow them to do it."

"Use 7 letters to spell **deplane**. The plane has landed and the passengers have started to **deplane**."

"Use 10 letters and make the word **dependable**. If someone can depend on you, you are **dependable**."

● Give the students one minute to figure out the secret word and then give clues if needed.

"Our secret word today is related to the word **depend**."

 Sort Related Words: bend, unbend; able, unable, enable; bundle, bundled;
plane, deplane; need, unneeded; lead, unleaded;
depend, dependable, undependable

● Draw students' attention to the words on index cards and have the words pronounced.

● Choose a set of related words and model for students how to use those words in sentences to show how they are related.

"Gasoline used to contain **lead** but when scientists found that **lead** was not safe, the formula was changed to produce gasoline without **lead** that is **unleaded**. The prefix **un** means not or the opposite."

● Let volunteers choose sets of related words and help them construct sentences and explain how the prefixes and suffixes change the root words.

 Transfer Words: repack, unpack; unstuck, stackable, restack; enact, react

● Have students use sorted words to spell other words. Be sure to have the class decide which related words to use and how to spell the new root word before letting anyone write the word. Let volunteers use new words in sentences that show meaning.

Lesson 25
disagreeable

Lesson Focus: **dis**, meaning not or opposite
er, meaning person or thing that does something
re, meaning back or again
able, meaning able to

Letters: | a | a | e | e | e | i | b | d | g | l | r | s |

 Make Words: lead/deal   able   seal/sale   read   erase   agree   leader/dealer
reseal/resale   desire   disable   erasable   readable   disagree
agreeable   desirable   disagreeable

Directions: Tell students how many letters to use to make each word.

- Emphasize how changing a few letters or rearranging letters makes different words. Words that can be spelled with the same letters are indicated by a /.

- Give meaning or sentence clues to clarify the word the students are making:

    "Use the same letters in **lead** to spell **deal**. Will you **deal** the cards?"

    "Use 6 letters and spell **leader**. A **leader** leads or guides a group."

    "Change the letters around and **leader** becomes **dealer**. A person who passes out the cards is a **dealer**."

    "Use 9 letters and make the word **agreeable**. If everyone is **agreeable**, we will schedule the picnic for Sunday."

- Give the students one minute to figure out the secret word and then give clues if needed.

    "Our secret word today is related to the word **disagree**."

 Sort Related Words: lead, leader; deal, dealer; sale, resale; seal, reseal;
read, readable; erase, erasable; desire, desirable;
able, disable; agree, agreeable, disagree, disagreeable

- Draw students' attention to the words on index cards and have the words pronounced.

- Choose a set of related words and model for students how to use those words in sentences to show how they are related.

    "My brother and I **agree** on most things but we **disagree** about which baseball team is the greatest. Most days, I am in an **agreeable** mood but when I am sick, I feel quite **disagreeable**. The prefix **dis** often turns a word into its opposite meaning. The suffix **able** means able to."

- Let volunteers choose sets of related words and help them construct sentences and explain how the prefixes and suffixes change the root words.

Transfer Words: appear, disappear, reappear;
connect, disconnect, reconnect, connectable

- Have students use sorted words to spell other words. Be sure to have the class decide which related words to use and how to spell the new root word before letting anyone write the word. Let volunteers use new words in sentences that show meaning.

Lesson 26
disagreement

Lesson Focus: **er/est**, meaning more and most
dis, meaning not or opposite
ee, meaning person
ment, changing part of speech

Letters: <u>a</u> <u>e</u> <u>e</u> <u>e</u> <u>i</u> <u>d</u> <u>g</u> <u>m</u> <u>n</u> <u>r</u> <u>s</u> <u>t</u>

 Make Words: arm mean dine diner agree train disarm reside detain meaner meanest migrant migrate emigrate trainees disagree resident detainees agreement disagreement

Directions: Tell students how many letters to use to make each word.

* Emphasize how changing a few letters or rearranging letters makes different words.

* Give meaning or sentence clues to clarify the word the students are making:

  "Add a letter to **dine** and spell **diner**. Did you ever eat at that **diner**?"

  "Spell the 7 letter word **migrant**. A person who leaves one place to go to another is a **migrant**."

  "Use 8 letters to spell **trainees**. People in training are called **trainees**."

* Give the students one minute to figure out the secret word and then give clues if needed.

  "Our secret word today is related to the word **agree**."

 Sort Related Words: dine, diner; mean, meaner, meanest;
migrate, migrant, emigrant; reside, resident;
train, trainees; detain, detainee; arm, disarm;
agree, disagree, agreement, disagreement

* Draw students' attention to the words on index cards and have the words pronounced.

* Choose a set of related words and model for students how to use those words in sentences to show how they are related.

  "The president and the congress could not **agree** on an immigration bill. Their **disagreement** was confirmed when the congress passed a bill but the president vetoed it. Hopefully the next president will not **disagree** with the congress and an **agreement** on immigration can be reached. **Dis** is a prefix which changes a word to its opposite meaning. **Ment** is a suffix which changes how a word can be used in a sentence."

* Let volunteers choose sets of related words and help them construct sentences and explain how the prefixes and suffixes change the root words.

Transfer Words: arrange, rearrange, arrangement;
move, remove, movement; pave, pavement

● Have students use sorted words to spell other words. Be sure to have the class decide which related words to use and how to spell the new root word before letting anyone write the word. Let volunteers use new words in sentences that show meaning.

Lesson 27
reinforcements

Lesson Focus: **er/est**, meaning more and most
                re, meaning back or again
                er, meaning person or thing that does something
                ment, changing part of speech

Letters: <u>e</u>   <u>e</u>   <u>e</u>   <u>i</u>   <u>o</u>   <u>c</u>   <u>f</u>   <u>m</u>   <u>n</u>   <u>n</u>   <u>r</u>   <u>r</u>   <u>s</u>   <u>t</u>

 Make Words: rent   riot   form   soft   sift   nice   mine   miner   force
         nicer   nicest   sifter   softer   soften   reform   renters
         rioters   enforce   reinforce   reinforcements

Directions: Tell students how many letters to use to make each word.

- Emphasize how changing a few letters or rearranging letters makes different words.

- Give meaning or sentence clues to clarify the word the students are making:

    "Change a letter in **soft** and spell **sift**. My mother used to **sift** her flour, now it comes already sifted."

    "Change a letter in the word **softer** and you can make the word **soften**. If you leave the butter out of the refrigerator it will **soften**."

    "You have spelled the word **force**; now use 9 letters and make the word **reinforce**. If you **reinforce** something you make it stronger."

- Give the students one minute to figure out the secret word and then give clues if needed.

    "Our secret word today is related to the word **reinforce**."

 Sort Related Words: rent, renters; riot, rioters; sift, sifter; mine, miner;
                       soft, softer, soften; nice, nicer, nicest; form, reform;
                       force, enforce, reinforce, reinforcements

- Draw students' attention to the words on index cards and have the words pronounced.

- Choose a set of related words and model for students how to use those words in sentences to show how they are related.

    "**Force** is power or strength. To **enforce** is to give power to something. To **reinforce** is to make something stronger. **Reinforcements** are when people are brought in to make something stronger. The prefix **en** means to make or give. The suffix **ment** changes the way a word can be used in a sentence."

- Let volunteers choose sets of related words and help them construct sentences and explain how the prefixes and suffixes change the root words.

 Transfer Words: courage, encourage, encouragement; excite, excitement;
                    equip, equipment

- Have students use sorted words to spell other words. Be sure to have the class decide which related words to use and how to spell the new root word before letting anyone write the word. Let volunteers use new words in a sentences that show meaning.

Lesson 28

imperfectly

Lesson Focus: **ly**, changing part of speech
y, changing part of speech
re, meaning back or again
im, meaning not or opposite

Letters: e e i c f l m p r t y

Make Words: lit free firm type time timer relit crept creep
creepy freely firmly retype fierce perfect fiercely
perfectly imperfect imperfectly

Directions: Tell students how many letters to use to make each word.

- Emphasize how changing a few letters or rearranging letters makes different words.

- Give meaning or sentence clues to clarify the word the students are making:

  "Use 4 letters to make the word **free**. When you are **free** you are not restricted."

  "Add a letter to **creep** and you have **creepy**. If something is **creepy** it is scary!"

  "You have spelled the word **fierce**; now use 8 letters and make the word **fiercely**. The dog snarled **fiercely** at the robber."

  "Use 9 letters and spell **perfectly**. When you do something without making a mistake people may say you do it **perfectly**."

- Give the students one minute to figure out the secret word and then give clues if needed.

  "Our secret word today is related to the word **perfect**."

Sort Related Words: lit, relit; type, retype; crept, creep, creepy; time, timer;
free, freely; firm, firmly; fierce, fiercely;
perfect, perfectly, imperfect, imperfectly

- Draw students' attention to the words on index cards and have the words pronounced.

- Choose a set of related words and model for students how to use those words in sentences to show how they are related.

  "The dancer wanted to be **perfect** and dance **perfectly** and do nothing **imperfect** in his performance. He fell at the end of his dance and thus ended a **perfect** performance **imperfectly**. **Im** is a prefix that changes words to their opposite meaning. **Ly** is a suffix that changes the way a word is used in a sentence."

- Let volunteers choose sets of related words and help them construct sentences and explain how the prefixes and suffixes change the root words.

Transfer Words: personal, impersonal; patient, impatient, impatiently;
possible, impossible, impossibly

- Have students use sorted words to spell other words. Be sure to have the class decide which related words to use and how to spell the new root word before letting anyone write the word. Let volunteers use new words in sentences that show meaning.

Lesson 29
irresponsible

Lesson Focus: **less**, meaning less or without
re, meaning back or again
er, meaning person or thing that does something
ir, meaning opposite
ible, meaning able to

Letters: | e | e | i | i | o | b | l | n | p | r | r | s | s |

 Make Words: open ripe bone lose loser riper, ripen broil
sense opener/reopen prison broiler prisoner boneless
sensible response responsible irresponsible

Directions: Tell students how many letters to use to make each word.

- Emphasize how changing a few letters or rearranging letters makes different words. Words that can be spelled with the same letters are indicated by a /.

- Give meaning or sentence clues to clarify the word the students are making:

  "Add a letter to **lose** and you can spell **loser**. A person who loses is a **loser**."

  "Use 6 letters to spell **opener**. An **opener** is a tool to open something with."

  "Move the letters in **opener** around and you can spell **reopen**. When you open something again you **reopen** it."

  "You have spelled the word **response**; now use 11 letters and make the word **responsible**. A **responsible** person is a person you can trust."

- Give the students one minute to figure out the secret word and then give clues if needed.

  "Our secret word today is the opposite of **responsible**."

 Sort Related Words: lose, loser; broil, broiler; ripe, ripen, riper;
open, reopen, opener; prison, prisoner; bone, boneless;
sense, sensible; response, responsible, irresponsible

- Draw students' attention to the words on index cards and have the words pronounced.

- Choose a set of related words and model for students how to use those words in sentences to show how they are related.

  "**Sense** means having intelligence. **Sensible** means to be smart or intelligent. If you have good **sense** you will make **sensible** decisions. **Ible** is a suffix that means able to."

- Let volunteers choose sets of related words and help them construct sentences and explain how the prefixes and suffixes change the root words.

Transfer Words: regular, irregular; resist, resistible, irresistible; flex, flexible, inflexible

- Have students use sorted words to spell other words. Be sure to have the class decide which related words to use and how to spell the new root word before letting anyone write the word. Let volunteers use new words in sentences that show meaning.

Lesson 30
misunderstand

Lesson Focus: **dis**, meaning not or opposite
in, meaning not or opposite
un, meaning not or opposite
mis, meaning wrong or badly
er/est, meaning more/most

Letters: | a | e | i | u | d | d | m | n | n | r | s | s | t |

 Make Words: mad sad arm aid use read sane train insane disarm misuse madder sadder saddest maddest misread unaided untrained understand misunderstand

Directions: Tell students how many letters to use to make each word.

- Emphasize how changing a few letters or rearranging letters makes different words.

- Give meaning or sentence clues to clarify the word the students are making:

  "Change a letter in **mad** and you can spell **sad**. What makes you feel **sad**?"

  "Use 6 letters and spell **insane**. The opposite of **sane** is **insane**."

  "Change one letter in **madder** and you can spell **sadder**. I was **sad** when my cat ran away and even **sadder** when my dog died."

  "You have spelled the word **train**; now use 9 letters and make the word **untrained**. An **untrained** person is not trained."

- Give the students one minute to figure out the secret word and then give clues if needed.

  "Our secret word today is related to the word **understand**."

 Sort Related Words: mad, madder, maddest; sad, sadder, saddest; arm, disarm; sane, insane; aid, unaided; train, untrained; use, misuse; read, misread; understand, misunderstand

- Draw students' attention to the words on index cards and have the words pronounced.

- Choose a set of related words and model for students how to use those words in sentences to show how they are related.

  "Please don't **misunderstand** me. I would like to come to your house but I promised my aunt I would babysit. I hope you **understand** and will invite me again. The prefix **mis** often means wrong or badly."

- Let volunteers choose sets of related words and help them construct sentences and explain how the prefixes and suffixes change the root words.

 Transfer Words: treat, mistreat, treatment, mistreatment; misspell, mistrust

- Have students use sorted words to spell other words. Be sure to have the class decide which related words to use and how to spell the new root word before letting anyone write the word. Let volunteers use new words in sentences that show meaning.

Lesson 31

misunderstood

Lesson Focus: **dis**, meaning not or opposite
mis, meaning wrong or badly
en, changing part of speech

Letters: e i o o u d d m n r s s t

 Make Words: sun use hid hide side rise room tour mount
moist hidden misused tourism sunrise sunroom
dismount moisture understood misunderstood

Directions: Tell students how many letters to use to make each word.

- Emphasize how changing a few letters or rearranging letters makes different words.

- Give meaning or sentence clues to clarify the word the students make:

    "Add a letter to the word **hid** and you can spell **hide**. Where will you **hide**?"

    "Use 6 letters and spell **hidden**. The money was **hidden** from view."

    "Use 6 letters and make the word **misuse**. Do not **misuse** the computer."

    "You have spelled both **sun** and **rise**; now spell the 7 letter word **sunrise**. The **sunrise** was beautiful this morning."

    "Use 7 letters again and spell **sunroom**. The **sunroom** was every one's favorite room."

    "You have spelled the word **mount**; now use 8 letters and make the word **dismount**. To **dismount** is to get off a horse."

- Give the students one minute to figure out the secret word and then give clues if needed.

    "Our secret word today is related to the word **understood**."

 Sort Related Words: sun, room, sunroom; sun, rise, sunrise; hid, hide, hidden;
tour, tourism; moist, moisture; mount, dismount; use, misused;
understood, misunderstood

- Draw students' attention to the words on index cards and have the words pronounced.

- Choose a set of related words and model for students how to use those words in sentences to show how they are related.

    "I thought I **understood** how to do the math homework but I did it all wrong so I must have **misunderstood**. **Mis** is a prefix meaning badly or wrong."

- Let volunteers choose sets of related words and help them construct sentences and explain how the prefixes and suffixes change the root words.

 Transfer Words: mistreat, misbehave, mismanage; sadden, lighten, frighten

- Have students use sorted words to spell other words. Be sure to have the class decide which related words to use and how to spell the new root word before letting anyone write the word. Let volunteers use new words in sentences that show meaning.

Lesson 32
interactively

Lesson Focus: **inter**, meaning between
in, meaning not or opposite
ee, meaning person
ly, changing part of speech

Letters: a e e i i c l n r t t v y

 Make Words: act   real   vary   nice   nicer   train   react   active   create
reality   variety   trainee   creative   inactive   interact
creatively   creativity   interactive   interactively

Directions: Tell students how many letters to use to make each word.

• Emphasize how changing a few letters or rearranging letters makes different words.

• Give meaning or sentence clues to clarify the word the students make:

"Add a letter to the word **nice** and you can spell **nicer**. The weather is **nicer** today."

"Use 6 letters and spell **active**. He is an **active** little boy."

"Use 7 letters and spell **reality**. When it really happens it is a **reality**."

"You have spelled the word **active**; now use 8 letters and spell **inactive**. If something is not active it is **inactive**."

"Use 10 letters and spell **creatively**. I like to cook **creatively**."

• Give the students one minute to figure out the secret word and then give clues if needed.

"Our secret word today is related to the word **active**."

 Sort Related Words: real, reality; vary, various; nice, nicer; train, trainee;
create, creative, creatively, creativity;
act, react, active, inactive, interact, interactive, interactively

• Draw students' attention to the words on index cards and have the words pronounced.

• Choose a set of related words and model for students how to use those words in sentences to show how they are related.

"**Act** means to do something. **Active** means moving. **Inactive** is not moving. To **interact** means an action between two people or two objects. **Interactive** is when something can be interacted with. The boy could **act** nicely but was very **active**. When he was **inactive**, everyone thought he was sick. He likes to **interact** with electronic games; especially **interactive** ones. **Inter** is a prefix meaning between."

• Let volunteers choose sets of related words and help them construct sentences and explain how the prefixes and suffixes change the root words.

Transfer Words: expense, expensive, inexpensive; sense, sensitive, insensitive, politely; happily

- Have students use sorted words to spell other words. Be sure to have the class decide which related words to use and how to spell the new root word before letting anyone write the word. Let volunteers use new words in sentences that show meaning.

Lesson 33
interactions

Lesson Focus: **er/est**, meaning more and most
re, meaning back or again
inter, meaning between
in, meaning opposite
er/or/ist, meaning person or thing that does something
tion, changing part of speech

Letters: a e i i o c n n r s t t

 Make Words: art act scan sane nice nicer react toast actors
artist nicest insane contain toaster scanner reaction
interact container interactions

Directions: Tell students how many letters to use to make each word.

- Emphasize how changing a few letters or rearranging letters makes different words.

- Give meaning or sentence clues to clarify the word the students make:

    "Use 6 letters and spell **actors**. The **actors** act in the play."

    "You have spelled the word **art**; now use 6 letters and spell **artist**. A person who makes artwork is an **artist**."

    "Use 9 letters and spell **container**. We put the fruit punch in a **container**."

- Give the students one minute to figure out the secret word and then give clues if needed.

    "Our secret word today is related to the word **act**."

 Sort Related Words: **art, artist; nice, nicer, nicest; scan, scanner;**
toast, toaster; contain, container; sane, insane;
act, react, actors, reaction, interact, interactions

- Draw students' attention to the words on index cards and have the words pronounced.

- Choose a set of related words and model for students how to use those words in sentences to show how they are related.

    "A **toaster** warms the surface of the bread and it becomes **toast**. **Er** is a suffix meaning person or thing."

- Let volunteers choose sets of related words and help them construct sentences and explain how the prefixes and suffixes change the root words.

 Transfer Words: **interchange, internet, interview, review;**
active, inactive, interactive

- Have students use sorted words to spell other words. Be sure to have the class decide which related words to use and how to spell the new root word before letting anyone write the word. Let volunteers use new words in sentences that show meaning.

Lesson 34
international

Lesson Focus: **inter**, meaning between
in, meaning not or opposite
al, changing part of speech
tion, changing part of speech

Letters: a a e i i o l n n r t t

 Make Words: toe tore torn nail rent loan alter loaner rental nation toenail national tolerant intention intolerant alteration intentional international

Directions: Tell students how many letters to use to make each word.

- Emphasize how changing a few letters or rearranging letters makes different words.

- Give meaning or sentence clues to clarify the word the students make:

  "Add one letter to the word **toe** and you can spell **tore**. He **tore** his shirt when playing football."

  "Use 5 letters and make the word **alter**. To **alter** is to make a change."

  "You have spelled the word **nation**; now use 8 letters and spell **national**; if it has to do with the **nation** it is **national**. Thanksgiving is a **national** holiday."

  "Use 10 letters and spell the word **alteration**. If you change something you make an **alteration**. The **alteration** on the gown was done at the store by a seamstress."

- Give the students one minute to figure out the secret word and then give clues if needed.

  "Our secret word today is related to the word **nation**."

 Sort Related Words: tore, torn; rent, rental; loan, loaner; tolerant, intolerant; alter, alteration; intention, intentional; toe, nail, toenail; nation, national, international

- Draw students' attention to the words on index cards and have the words pronounced.

- Choose a set of related words and model for students how to use those words in sentences to show how they are related.

  "Our **nation** has a **national** government and we also belong to the United Nations, an **international** organization. The prefix **inter** means between. The suffix **al** changes how a word can be used in a sentence."

- Let volunteers choose sets of related words and help them construct sentences and explain how the prefixes and suffixes change the root words.

 Transfer Words: magic, magical; music, musical, arrive, arrival; survive, survival

- Have students use sorted words to spell other words. Be sure to have the class decide which related words to use and how to spell the new root word before letting anyone write the word. Let volunteers use new words in sentences that show meaning.

Lesson 35
mysteriously

Lesson Focus: **mis**, meaning wrong or badly
y, changing part of speech
ly, changing part of speech
ous, changing part of speech

Letters: | e̲ i̲ o̲ u̲ l̲ m̲ r̲ s̲ s̲ t̲ y̲ y̲ |

 Make Words: use tour sure mess messy slime slimy moist storm stormy surely misuse tourism mystery serious seriously moisture mysterious mysteriously

Directions: Tell students how many letters to use to make each word.

- Emphasize how changing a few letters or rearranging letters makes different words.

- Give meaning or sentence clues to clarify the word the students make:

    "Add one letter to the word **mess** and you can spell **messy**. He is very **messy** when he cooks."

    "Use 6 letters and make the word **surely**. You can **surely** do that."

    "Use 7 letters to spell **mystery**. I am reading a wonderful **mystery**."

    "You have spelled the word **mystery**; now use 10 letters and spell **mysterious**. If something is a mystery it is **mysterious**."

- Give the students one minute to figure out the secret word and then give clues if needed.

    "Our secret word today is related to the word **mystery**."

 Sort Related Words: **mess, messy; slime, slimy; storm, stormy; moist, moisture; tour, tourism; use, misuse; sure, surely; serious, seriously; mystery, mysterious, mysteriously**

- Draw students' attention to the words on index cards and have the words pronounced.

- Choose a set of related words and model for students how to use those words in sentences to show how they are related.

    "It is still a **mystery** what happened to the presents that **mysteriously** disappeared just before my birthday and no one can explain their **mysterious** reappearance. **Ous** and **ly** are suffixes that change where a word can be used in a sentence."

- Let volunteers choose sets of related words and help them construct sentences and explain how the prefixes and suffixes change the root words.

 Transfer Words: **joy, joyous, joyously; danger, dangerous, dangerously**

- Have students use sorted words to spell other words. Be sure to have the class decide which related words to use and how to spell the new root word before letting anyone write the word. Let volunteers use new words in sentences that show meaning.

Lesson 36
dangerously

Lesson Focus: **un**, meaning not or opposite
re, meaning back or again
ly, changing part of speech
ous, changing part of speech

Letters: | a | e | o | u | d | g | l | n | r | s | y |

 Make Words: do redo undo load real seal easy near sugar
sugary reload unload unreal unseal uneasy nearly
danger dangerous dangerously

Directions: Tell students how many letters to use to make each word.

- Emphasize how changing a few letters or rearranging letters makes different words.

- Give meaning or sentence clues to clarify the word the students make:

    "Add 2 letters to **do** and make the word **redo**. I will **redo** my bedroom in my favorite colors."

    "Change 2 letters and you can spell **undo**. I cannot **undo** this knot."

    "Add one letter to **sugar** and make **sugary**. The sticky bun was **sugary** sweet."

    "Add 3 letters to **danger** and spell the word **dangerous**. Being in a boat during a storm is very **dangerous**."

- Give the students one minute to figure out the secret word and then give clues if needed.

    "Our secret word today is related to the word **danger**."

 Sort Related Words: do, redo, undo; load, reload, unload; seal, unseal;
real, unreal; easy, uneasy; sugar, sugary; near, nearly;
danger, dangerous, dangerously

- Draw students' attention to the words on index cards and have the words pronounced.

- Choose a set of related words and model for students how to use those words in sentences.

    "Police officers are often in **dangerous** situations. **Danger** lurks around every corner. Do you think they like living **dangerously**? **Ous** and **ly** are suffixes that change where a word can be used in a sentence."

- Let volunteers choose sets of related words and help them construct sentences and explain how the prefixes and suffixes change the root words.

 Transfer Words: **proudly, wildly, loudly, softly; fame, famous, famously**

- Have students use sorted words to spell other words. Be sure to have the class decide which related words to use and how to spell the new root word before letting anyone write the word. Let volunteers use new words in sentences that show meaning.

Lesson 37
independently

Lesson Focus: **in**, meaning not or opposite (independent)
in, meaning in (indent)
en, meaning to make
y, changing part of speech
ly, changing part of speech

Letters: e̲ e̲ e̲ i̲ d̲ d̲ l̲ n̲ n̲ n̲ p̲ t̲ y̲

 Make Words: lid eye dent deep nine need needy eyelid ninety
depend indent deeply deepen nineteen dependent
independent independently

Directions: Tell students how many letters to use to make each word.

- Emphasize how changing a few letters or rearranging letters makes different words.

- Give meaning or sentence clues to clarify the word the students make:

   "Add a letter to **need** and you can spell **needy**. The woman looked very **needy**."

   "Change 2 letters in **deeply** and spell the word **deepen**. His voice will **deepen** as he gets older."

   "Use 8 letters and spell the word **dependent**. A person who is **dependent** relies or depends on someone else."

   "Add 2 letters to **dependent** and spell the word **independent**. Someone who is not dependent is **independent**."

- Give the students one minute to figure out the secret word and then give clues if needed.

   "Our secret word today is related to the word **depend**."

 Sort Related Words: dent, indent; nine, nineteen, ninety; need, needy;
lid, eye, eyelid; deep, deepen, deeply;
depend, independent, independently

- Draw students' attention to the words on index cards and have the words pronounced.

- Choose a set of related words and model for students how to use those words in sentences.

   "Babies **depend** on their parents for everything. Babies are very **dependent** on their parents but as they get older, they get more **independent**. **In** is a prefix that sometimes means the opposite."

- Let volunteers choose sets of related words and help them construct sentences and explain how the prefixes and suffixes change the root words.

Transfer Words: widely, widen; written, unwritten; sixty, sixteen; seventy, seventeen

- Have students use sorted words to spell other words. Be sure to have the class decide which related words to use and how to spell the new root word before letting anyone write the word. Let volunteers use new words in sentences that show meaning.

Lesson 38
dependability

Lesson Focus: **in**, meaning opposite
en, changing part of speech
y, changing part of speech
ly, changing part of speech

Letters: a e e i i b d d l n p t y

 Make Words: bad eat beat neat able deep need needy badly
eaten beaten neatly deeply depend edible ability
inedible dependability

Directions: Tell students how many letters to use to make each word.

- Emphasize how changing a few letters or rearranging letters makes different words.

- Give meaning or sentence clues to clarify the word the students make:

   "Add a letter to **eat** and spell **beat**. I like to **beat** the eggs when making a cake."

   "Add a letter to **eaten** and make the 6 letter word **beaten**. The eggs need to be **beaten** before they are added to the cake mixture."

   "Make the 6 letter word **edible**. If you can eat it, it is **edible**."

   "Use 7 letters and spell the word **ability**. If you are able to do it you have the **ability**."

   "You have spelled **edible**; now use 8 letters and make the word **inedible**. Something that is **inedible** cannot be eaten."

- Give the students one minute to figure out the secret word and then give clues if needed.

   "Our secret word today is related to the word **depend**."

 Sort Related Words: **eat, eaten; beat, beaten; deep, deeply; bad, badly;
neat, neatly; need, needy; edible, inedible; able, ability;
depend, ability, dependability**

- Draw students' attention to the words on index cards and have the words pronounced.

- Choose a set of related words and model for students how to use those words in sentences.

   "Some mushrooms are **edible** but other mushrooms are poisonous and are **inedible**. The prefix **in** sometimes changes a word to its opposite meaning."

- Let volunteers choose sets of related words and help them construct sentences and explain how the prefixes and suffixes change the root words.

 Transfer Words: **invalid, intolerant; broken, straighten; itchy, scratchy;
angrily, bravely**

- Have students use sorted words to spell other words. Be sure to have the class decide which related words to use and how to spell the new root word before letting anyone write the word. Let volunteers use new words in sentences that show meaning.

Lesson 39

encouragement

Lesson Focus: **er/or**, meaning person
re, meaning back or again
en, meaning to make
ment, changing part of speech

Letters: | a e e e o u c g m n n r t |

 Make Words: eat   act   age   rage   actor   react   enact   agree   argue
eaten   enrage   uneaten   courage   outrage   teenager
argument   agreement   encourage   encouragement

Directions: Tell students how many letters to use to make each word.

● Emphasize how changing a few letters or rearranging letters makes different words.

● Give meaning or sentence clues to clarify the word the students make:

"Use 5 letters to spell **react**. How did he **react** to the bad news?"

"Change 2 letters in **react** and spell the word **enact**. The government failed to **enact** the law giving health insurance to all children."

"Use 6 letters and spell the word **enrage**. If you **enrage** someone, you make them extremely angry."

● Give the students one minute to figure out the secret word and then give clues if needed.

"Our secret word today is related to the word **courage**."

 Sort Related Words: eat, eaten, uneaten; act, actor, react, enact;
rage, enrage, outrage; age, teenager; argue, argument;
agree, agreement; courage, encourage, encouragement

● Draw students' attention to the words on index cards and have the words pronounced.

● Choose a set of related words and model for students how to use those words in sentences.

"If you have **courage**, you aren't afraid. When you **encourage** someone, you give **encouragement**. The prefix **en** sometimes means make or give. The suffix **ment** changes how a word can be used in a sentence."

● Let volunteers choose sets of related words and help them construct sentences and explain how the prefixes and suffixes change the root words.

 Transfer Words: discourage, disagreement, payment, settlement,
measurement, assignment

● Have students use sorted words to spell other words. Be sure to have the class decide which related words to use and how to spell the new root word before letting anyone write the word. Let volunteers use new words in sentences that show meaning.

Lesson 40
arrangements

Lesson Focus: **er/est**, meaning more/most
re, meaning back or again
er, meaning person
ment, changing part of speech

Letters: a a e e g m n n r r s t

 Make Words: arm   name/mean   near   rest   smart   rearm   rename/meaner
nearer   manage   manager   nearest   meanest   smarter
armrest   arrange   arrangements

Directions: Tell students how many letters to use to make each word.

- Emphasize how changing a few letters or rearranging letters makes different words. Words that can be spelled with the same letters are indicated by a /.

- Give meaning or sentence clues to clarify the word the students make:

  "Use 3 letters and make the word **arm**. Did you hurt your **arm**?"

  "Use 6 letters and spell **rename**. When you give someone a new name you **rename** him or her."

  "Move the letters around in **rename** and spell **meaner**. He was the **meaner** of the two."

  "Using 7 letters make the word **armrest**. A place on a chair where you rest your arm is an **armrest**."

- Give the students one minute to figure out the secret word and then give clues if needed.

  "Our secret word today is related to the word **arrange**."

 Sort Related Words: arm, rearm; arm, rest, armrest; name, rename;
near, nearer, nearest; smart, smarter; mean, meaner, meanest;
manage, manager; arrange, arrangements

- Draw students' attention to the words on index cards and have the words pronounced.

- Choose a set of related words and model for students how to use those words in sentences.

  "If you are close by you are **near**. If you are closer than that then you are **nearer**. The closest person is the **nearest**." **Er** and **est** are suffixes meaning more and most."

- Let volunteers choose sets of related words and help them construct sentences and explain how the prefixes and suffixes change the root words.

70

Transfer Words: sweet, sweeter, sweetest; rewrite, replay; teacher, farmer; unemployment, entertainment

- Have students use sorted words to spell other words. Be sure to have the class decide which related words to use and how to spell the new root word before letting anyone write the word. Let volunteers use new words in sentences that show meaning.

Lesson 41

replacements

Lesson Focus: **er/est**, meaning more/most
re, meaning back or again
er, meaning person
al, changing part of speech
ment, changing part of speech

Letters:

a	e	e	e	c	l	m	n	p	r	s	t

 Make Words: act camp calm react place steam elect sleep
asleep calmer center central calmest replace
reelect campers steamer placement replacements

Directions: Tell students how many letters to use to make each word.

- Emphasize how changing a few letters or rearranging letters makes different words.

- Give meaning or sentence clues to clarify the word the students make:

  "Use 5 letters and spell the word **sleep**. Every night we **sleep**."

  "Add a letter to **sleep** and spell **asleep**. Is the baby **asleep**?"

  "Use 6 letters and spell **center**. We sat in the **center** or middle of the room."

  "Using 7 letters make the word **central**. We met at a **central** location."

  "Use 7 letters again and spell **campers**. The **campers** returned to camp."

- Give the students one minute to figure out the secret word and then give clues if needed.

  "Our secret word today is related to the word **place**."

 Sort Related Words: **act, react; camp, campers;**
calm, calmer, calmest; steam, steamer;
elect, reelect; sleep, asleep; center, central;
place, replace, placement, replacements

- Draw students' attention to the words on index cards and have the words pronounced.

- Choose a set of related words and model for students how to use those words in sentences.

  "I am going to **place** the dishes here on the table so people can serve themselves. Help me think about the **placement** of the food so that people can easily reach it. Last time we had a party, I broke a dish and I need to **replace** it. **Replacement** dishes are expensive. The prefix **re** means back or again. The suffix **ment** changes how a word can be used in a sentence."

- Let volunteers choose sets of related words and help them construct sentences and explain how the prefixes and suffixes change the root words.

Transfer Words: happy, happier, happiest; reprint, rework; driver, player; personal; government

- Have students use sorted words to spell other words. Be sure to have the class decide which related words to use and how to spell the new root word before letting anyone write the word. If needed, remind the students to change the **y** to an **i** before adding the endings. Let volunteers use new words in sentences that show meaning.

Lesson 42
underweight

Lesson Focus: **under**, meaning under or less
re, meaning back or again
er, meaning person or thing that does something
er, meaning more

Letters: e e i u d g h n r t w

 Make Words: new hunt diet/tied wide wider widen weigh renew
under untie/unite united untied retied hunter dieter
weight reunite underweight

Directions: Tell students how many letters to use to make each word.

- Emphasize how changing a few letters or rearranging letters makes different words. Words that can be spelled with the same letters are indicated by a /.

- Give meaning or sentence clues to clarify the word the students make:

   "Use 4 letters and spell **wide**. The bridge was **wide** enough for two cars to go through."

   "Add one letter to **wide** and spell **wider**. Many people thought the bridge should have been **wider**."

   "Change 1 letter and spell **widen**. Who will **widen** the bridge?"

   "Use 5 letters to make the word **untie**. He will **untie** his shoes before taking them off."

   "Move the letters in **untie** to spell **unite**. To get together is to **unite**."

- Give the students one minute to figure out the secret word and then give clues if needed.

   "Our secret word today is related to the word **weight**."

 Sort Related Words: new, renew; tied, untie, untied, retied; unite, united, reunite; wide, wider, widen; hunt, hunter; diet, dieter; weigh, weight, under, underweight

- Draw students' attention to the words on index cards and have the words pronounced.

- Choose a set of related words and model for students how to use those words in sentences.

   "To get together is to **unite**. When the states got together they **united**. If they separated and get back together they will **reunite**. The prefix **re** means back or again."

- Let volunteers choose sets of related words and help them construct sentences and explain how the prefixes and suffixes change the root words.

Transfer Words: underwear, understudy; reproduce, reload;
fighter, singer; higher

- Have students use sorted words to spell other words. Be sure to have the class decide which related words to use and how to spell the new root word before letting anyone write the word. Let volunteers use new words in sentences that show meaning.

Lesson 43
underestimate

Lesson Focus: **under**, meaning under or less
re, meaning back or again
ee, meaning person
mis, meaning wrong or badly
en, meaning to make

Letters: | a e e e i u d m n r s t t |

 Make Words: sea name mate sure dear admit treat train detain inmate ensure endear rename readmit trainee detainee mistreat undersea estimate underestimate

Directions: Tell students how many letters to use to make each word.

- Emphasize how changing a few letters or rearranging letters makes different words.

- Give meaning or sentence clues to clarify the word the students make:

    "Use 5 letters and spell the word **admit**. A ticket will **admit** you to the show."

    "Use 6 letters and spell **detain**. To **detain** means to hold back. They will **detain** us if we are late."

    "You have spelled **admit**; use 7 letters and spell **readmit**. They will **readmit** you to the park if you have a stamp on your hand."

    "Use 7 letters and spell the word **trainee**. Each **trainee** gets lots of help to learn the job."

- Give the students one minute to figure out the secret word and then give clues if needed.

    "Our secret word today is related to the word **estimate**."

 Sort Related Words: dear, endear; sure, ensure; name, rename; admit, readmit; train, trainee; detain, detainee; mate, inmate; treat, mistreat; sea, undersea; estimate, underestimate

- Draw students' attention to the words on index cards and have the words pronounced.

- Choose a set of related words and model for students how to use those words in sentences.

    "The suspect was under arrest and was **detained** until court opened in the morning. The judge decided there was not enough evidence to hold him so the **detainee** was let go. The suffix **ee** means a person."

- Let volunteers choose sets of related words and help them construct sentences and explain how the prefixes and suffixes change the root words.

Transfer Words: employee, trainee, amputee, refugee;
underage, underdog, underground

- Have students use sorted words to spell other words. Be sure to have the class decide which related words to use and how to spell the new root word before letting anyone write the word. Let volunteers use new words in sentences that show meaning.

Lesson 44
overestimate

Lesson Focus: **over**, meaning over or more
er, meaning person or thing that does something

Letters: | a e e e i o m r s t t v |

 Make Words: time move vote voter timer toast steam movers
movies remove meteor motive toaster steamer motivate
estimate overtime meteorite overestimate

Directions: Tell students how many letters to use to make each word.

- Emphasize how changing a few letters or rearranging letters makes different words.

- Give meaning or sentence clues to clarify the word the students make:

    "Use 4 letters and spell the word **vote**. Who will you **vote** for?"

    "Add 1 letter and spell the word **voter**. A **voter** is a person who votes."

    "Use 6 letters and spell **movers**. The **movers** will be here soon."

    "Use 8 letters and spell the word **estimate**. To **estimate** is to make a rough calculation. I will **estimate** how much money I will need for the trip."

- Give the students one minute to figure out the secret word and then give clues if needed.

    "Our secret word today is related to the word **estimate**."

 Sort Related Words: time, timer, overtime; vote, voter;
move, movers, movies, remove; toast, toaster; steam, steamer;
meteor, meteorite; motive, motivate; estimate, overestimate

- Draw students' attention to the words on index cards and have the words pronounced.

- Choose a set of related words and model for students how to use those words in sentences.

    "**Time** means a duration or period. A **timer** keeps track of **time**. If you work **overtime** you work more time than your regular hours. The suffix **er** sometimes means a person or thing that does something. The prefix **over** means over or more."

- Let volunteers choose sets of related words and help them construct sentences and explain how the prefixes and suffixes change the root words.

 Transfer Words: overcook, overcoat, overdue, oversleep;
banker, trucker, hiker

- Have students use sorted words to spell other words. Be sure to have the class decide which related words to use and how to spell the new root word before letting anyone write the word. Let volunteers use new words in sentences that show meaning.

Lesson 45
performances

Lesson Focus: **en**, meaning to make
er, meaning person or thing that does something
ance, changing part of speech

Letters: | a e e o c f m n p r r s |

 Make Words: camp   case   farm   form   name   erase   eraser   encase
reform   rename   scrape   scraper   farmers   campers
perform   performances

Directions: Tell students how many letters to use to make each word.

- Emphasize how changing a few letters or rearranging letters makes different words.

- Give meaning or sentence clues to clarify the word the students make:

    "Change 1 letter in **farm** to spell **form**. Have you filled out your **form** for school?"

    "Use 5 letters and spell **erase**. Please **erase** the whiteboard for me."

    "Add a letter to **erase** and you have **eraser**. It is helpful to have an **eraser** on your pencil."

    "Add a letter to **scrape** and spell the word **scraper**. I need a **scraper** to clear my windows."

- Give the students one minute to figure out the secret word and then give clues if needed.

    "Our secret word today is related to the word **perform**."

 Sort Related Words: camp, **campers**; farm, **farmers**; erase, **erasers**;
scrape, **scrapers**; case, **encase**; name, **rename**;
form, **reform**; perform, **performances**

- Draw students' attention to the words on index cards and have the words pronounced.

- Choose a set of related words and model for students how to use those words in sentences.

    "When you **form** something, you make it a certain way or shape. When you **reform** something, you change it to make it better. To **perform** means to do something. When you **perform** in a play, you are part of the **performance**. The suffix **ance** changes how a word can be used in a sentence."

- Let volunteers choose sets of related words and help them construct sentences and explain how the prefixes and suffixes change the root words.

 Transfer Words: clearance, attendance, importance, appearance,
disappearance, insurance

- Have students use sorted words to spell other words. Be sure to have the class decide which related words use and how to spell the new root word before letting anyone write the word. Let volunteers use new words in sentences that show meaning.

Lesson 46

resistance

Lesson Focus: **er/est**, meaning more/most
re, meaning back or again
en, meaning to make
er/ee, meaning person
ance, changing part of speech

Letters: a e e i c n r s s t

 Make Words: eat act nice neat east react enact train nicer nicest neater eaters resist eastern actress reenact trainees resistance

Directions: Tell students how many letters to use to make each word.

- Emphasize how changing a few letters or rearranging letters makes different words.

- Give meaning or sentence clues to clarify the word the students make:

    "Use 4 letters and spell the word **neat**. I always try to be **neat**."

    "Use 5 letters and spell the word **react**. How did you **react** to the news?"

    "Change 2 letters in **react** to spell **enact**. To **enact** is to pass a law. The government will **enact** an important law this week."

    "Use 7 letters and spell **actress**. Who is your favorite **actress** in that movie?"

- Give the students one minute to figure out the secret word and then give clues if needed.

    "Our secret word today is related to the word **resist**."

 Sort Related Words: eat, eaters; train, trainees; act, actress; nice, nicer, nicest; neat, neater; east, eastern; act, react, enact, reenact; resist, resistance

- Draw students' attention to the words on index cards and have the words pronounced.

- Choose a set of related words and model for students how to use those words in sentences.

    "I was dieting and trying to **resist** the temptation to eat desserts. My **resistance** failed when my friend baked a chocolate cake. The suffix **ance** changes how a word can be used in a sentence."

- Let volunteers choose sets of related words and help them construct sentences and explain how the prefixes and suffixes change the root words.

 Transfer Words: guidance, endurance, annoyance, allowance, acceptance, disturbance

- Have students use sorted words to spell other words. Be sure to have the class decide which related words to use and how to spell the new root word before letting anyone write the word. Let volunteers use new words in sentences that show meaning.

disappearance

Lesson Focus: **dis**, meaning not or opposite
pre, meaning before
en, meaning to make
er, meaning person or thing that does something
ance, changing part of speech

Letters: <u>a</u> <u>a</u> <u>a</u> <u>e</u> <u>e</u> <u>i</u> <u>c</u> <u>d</u> <u>n</u> <u>p</u> <u>p</u> <u>r</u> <u>s</u>

Make Words: dip ripe sand dear case paid paper ripen dance
dancer dipper endear encase appear prepaid sandpaper
disappear appearance disappearance

Directions: Tell students how many letters to use to make each word.

- Emphasize how changing a few letters or rearranging letters makes different words.

- Give meaning or sentence clues to clarify the word the students make:

    "Use 5 letters again and spell the word **ripen**. To **ripen** the fruit you need lots of sunshine."

    "Use 5 letters and spell **dance**. When did you learn to **dance** like that?"

    "Add one letter to **dance** and you can make **dancer**. Sasha is the best **dancer** on the show."

    "Use 7 letters and spell **prepaid**. I **prepaid** my hotel for a better rate."

- Give the students one minute to figure out the secret word and then give clues if needed.

    "Our secret word today is related to the word **appear**."

Sort Related Words: dear, endear; case, encase; paid, prepaid; dip, dipper;
dance, dancer; ripe, ripen; sand, paper, sandpaper;
appear, disappear, appearance, disappearance

- Draw students' attention to the words on index cards and have the words pronounced.

- Choose a set of related words and model for students how to use those words in sentences.

    "When I went to pay for my tickets, the clerk told me they had been **prepaid**. As a birthday surprise, my mom had already **paid** for my tickets and didn't tell me. The prefix **pre** sometimes means before."

- Let volunteers choose sets of related words and help them construct sentences and explain how the prefixes and suffixes change the root words.

Transfer Words: disapprove, disagree; preview, precaution, premature;
enlarge, enrage

- Have students use sorted words to spell other words. Be sure to have the class decide which related words to use and how to spell the new root word before letting anyone write the word. Let volunteers use new words in sentences that show meaning.

Lesson 48
predictions/description

Lesson Focus: **er/or**, meaning person
er/est, meaning more/most
tion, changing part of speech

Letters: e i i o c d n p r s t

 Make Words: ice   nice   edit   point   scoot   nicer   nicest   iciest   direct
editor   predict   pointer   scooter   inspect   inspector
directions   predictions/description

Directions: Tell students how many letters to use to make each word.

- Emphasize how changing a few letters or rearranging letters makes different words. Words that can be spelled with the same letters are indicated by a /.

- Give meaning or sentence clues to clarify the word the students make:

  "Add one letter to **ice** and spell the word **nice**. Be **nice** to your classmates."

  "Use 5 letters and spell the word **point**. Is there a **point** on the end of your pencil?"

  "Use 6 letters and spell **nicest**. I think she is the **nicest** teacher at school."

  "Use 7 letters and spell **predict**. I **predict** the weather will be warmer next week."

  "Use 9 letters and spell **inspector**. He is an **inspector** at the laboratory."

  "Use all the letters and spell the secret words. There are two secret words today."

- Give the students one minute to figure out the secret words and then give clues if needed.

  "One secret word today is related to the word **predict**. The other secret word you can make with the same letters is related to the word **describe**."

 Sort Related Words: nice, nicer, nicest; ice, iciest; point, pointer;
scoot, scooter; edit, editor; inspect, inspector;
direct, directions; predict, predictions

- Draw students' attention to the words on index cards and have the words pronounced.

- Choose a set of related words and model for students how to use those words in sentences.

  "The health **inspector** goes to all the restaurants to **inspect** them and make sure they are clean. The suffix **or** sometimes means a person."

- Let volunteers choose sets of related words and help them construct sentences and explain how the prefixes and suffixes change the root words.

Transfer Words: action, attention, construction, production, attraction, subtraction

- Have students use sorted words to spell other words. Be sure to have the class decide which related words to use and how to spell the new root word before letting anyone write the word. Let volunteers use new words in sentences that show meaning.

Lesson 49
reproduction

Lesson Focus: **er/or**, meaning person
un, meaning not or opposite
re, meaning back or again
tion, changing part of speech

Letters: | e | i | o | o | u | c | d | n | p | r | r | t |

 Make Words: turn tied edit print untied return editor direct
printer/reprint corrupt product produce producer director
reproduce corruption production reproduction

Directions: Tell students how many letters to use to make each word.

- Emphasize how changing a few letters or rearranging letters makes different words. Words that can be spelled with the same letters are indicated by a /.

- Give meaning or sentence clues to clarify the word the students make:

  "Use 7 letters and spell the word **printer**. The **printer** is on my desk."

  "Move the letters around and spell **reprint**. I will **reprint** the pictures so my sister can have copies."

  "Add a letter to **produce** and spell **producer**. He is a famous **producer** of movies."

- Give the students one minute to figure out the secret word and then give clues if needed.

  "Our secret word today is related to the word **produce**."

 Sort Related Words: turn, return; print, printer, reprint; tied, untied;
edit, editor; direct, director; corrupt, corruption;
produce, product, producer, production, reproduce,
reproduction

- Draw students' attention to the words on index cards and have the words pronounced.

- Choose a set of related words and model for students using those words in sentences.

  "When you **produce** something, you make it. The thing you make is called the **product** and the person making the **product** is the **producer**. When you make something again, you **reproduce** it. **Production** and **reproduction** are the processes used for **producing** and **reproducing** things. The prefix **re** means back or again. The suffix **er** means a person or thing. The suffix **tion** changes how the word can be used in the sentence."

- Let volunteers choose sets of related words and help them construct sentences and explain how the prefixes and suffixes change the root words.

Transfer Words: construction, reconstruction, adoption, distraction, restriction, prevention

- Have students use sorted words to spell other words. Be sure to have the class decide which related words to use and how to spell the new root word before letting anyone write the word. Let volunteers use new words in sentences that show meaning.

Lesson 50

contradictions

Lesson Focus: **or/ist**, meaning person
tion, changing part of speech

Letters: $\underline{a} \quad \underline{i} \quad \underline{i} \quad \underline{o} \quad \underline{o} \quad \underline{c} \quad \underline{c} \quad \underline{d} \quad \underline{n} \quad \underline{n} \quad \underline{r} \quad \underline{s} \quad \underline{t} \quad \underline{t}$

 Make Words: art act actor action artist nation nations distort
distract contract cartoons artistic cartoonist distortion
distraction contradict contractions contradictions

Directions: Tell students how many letters to use to make each word.

- Emphasize how changing a few letters or rearranging letters makes different words.

- Give meaning or sentence clues to clarify the word the students make:

  "Add 2 letters to **act** and spell the word **actor**. Who is your favorite **actor**?"

  "Use 6 letters and spell the word **action**. The movie had lots of **action**."

  "Use 8 letters and spell **distract**. Do not **distract** me while I am writing."

  "Use 10 letters and spell **distortion**. The picture was a **distortion** of what the building really looked like."

- Give the students one minute to figure out the secret word and then give clues if needed.

  "Our secret word today is related to the word **contradict**."

 Sort Related Words: act, actor, action; nation, nations; art, artist, artistic;
cartoons, cartoonist; contract, contractions;
distract, distraction; distort, distortion;
contradict, contradictions.

- Draw students' attention to the words on index cards and have the words pronounced.

- Choose a set of related words and model for students how to use those words in sentences.

  "I love to draw **cartoons** and when I grow up I want to be a **cartoonist**. The suffix **ist** sometimes means a person."

- Let volunteers choose sets of related words and help them construct sentences and explain how the prefixes and suffixes change the root words.

 Transfer Words: cyclist, organist, pianist; donation, collection, protection

- Have students use sorted words to spell other words. Be sure to have the class decide which related words to use and how to spell the new root word before letting anyone write the word. Let volunteers use new words in sentences that show meaning.

Reproducible Letter Strips

1. a e e e o l m n r s t w _ _ _ _

2. a e i c d d g h l n n r r _ _ _

3. a e e e e c d h l r r s _ _ _

4. a a e e u h k q t r s _ _ _

5. e i i f g n n p r r s t _ _ _

6. a a e u b c k q r r s t ___ ___ ___ ___ ___ ___ ___ ___ ___ ___ ___ ___

7. a e i c g h h l r s t ___ ___ ___ ___ ___ ___ ___ ___ ___ ___ ___

8. a a e i u l m n p r t ___ ___ ___ ___ ___ ___ ___ ___ ___ ___ ___

9. e i u d f l n n r y ___ ___ ___ ___ ___ ___ ___ ___ ___ ___

10. e e i i t u d f l n n r s t ___ ___ ___ ___ ___ ___ ___ ___ ___ ___ ___ ___ ___ ___

11. e e i i u d f l n n r s s _ _ _ _ _

12. a e i o l n p r s t y _ _ _ _ _ _

13. a e e c l l i r s s y _ _ _ _ _ _

14. a e e i g l m n n s s _ _ _ _ _ _

15. e e i c l l m r s s y _ _ _ _ _ _

16. a e u c f g l l r y
    a _ _ _ _ _ g _ _ y

17. a e o u u f l n n r t t y
    a _ _ _ _ _ _ _ t _ y

18. a e o u b k l n r w
    a _ _ _ _ _

19. a a e e u b b k l n r
    a _ _ _ _ _ _

20. a e e i u b d l n r s
    a _ _ _ _ _

21. a e e i o u b l n q s t ___
22. a e e i u b c d l n p r t ___
23. a e o o u b c f l m n r t ___
24. a e e e u b d d l n n p ___
25. a a e e e i b d g l r s ___

26. a e e e i d **g** m n r s t ___ ___

27. e e e i o c f m n n r r s **t** ___

28. e e i c f l m p r t **y** ___

29. e e i i o b l n p **r** r s s ___

30. a e i u d d m n n r s s t ___

31. e i o o u d d m n r s s t _ _ _ _

32. a e e i i c l n r t t v y _ _ _ _

33. a e i i o c n n n r s t t _ _ _ _

34. a a e i i o l n n n r t t _ _ _ _

35. e i o u l m r s s t y y _ _ _ _

36. a e o u d g l n r s y ___

37. e e e i d d l n n n p t y ___

38. a e e i i b d d l n p t y ___

39. a e e e o u c g m n n r t ___

40. a a e e g m n n n r r s t ___

41. a e e c l m n p r s t ___ ___ ___ ___ ___ ___

42. e e i u d g h n r t w ___ ___ ___

43. a e e e i u d m n r s t t ___ ___ ___ ___ ___

44. a e e e i o m r s t t v ___ ___ ___ ___ ___

45. a e e o c f m n p r r s ___ ___ ___ ___ ___

46. a e e i c n r s s t   _ _ _ _ _ _ _ _ _ _

47. a a a e e i c d n p p r s   _ _ _ _ _ _ _ _ _ _ _ _ _

48. e i i o c d n p r s t   _ _ _ _ _ _ _ _ _ _ _

49. e i o o u c d n p r r t   _ _ _ _ _ _ _ _ _ _ _ _

50. a i i o o c c d n n r s t t   _ _ _ _ _ _ _ _ _ _ _ _ _ _

Reproducible Making Words Take-Home Sheet